FLATLINE TO CHANGE

FLATLINE TO CHANGE

Identity, Reality, Conflict, Engagement

Michael Gaffley, EdD

Library of Congress Control Number: 2009910682
ISBN: Hardcover 978-1-4415-8849-4
Softcover 978-1-4415-8848-7

This book was printed in the United States of America.

To order additional copies of this book, contact:
Xlibris Corporation
1-888-795-4274
www.Xlibris.com
Orders@Xlibris.com

68549

CONTENTS

My grandmother's credo was in the words of Maxwell N. Cornelius.

Not now, but in the coming years,
It may be in the better land,
We'll read the meaning of our tears,
And there, some time, we'll understand.

Then trust in God through all the days;
Fear not, for He doth hold thy hand;
Though dark thy way, still sing and praise,
Some time, some time we'll understand.

We'll catch the broken thread again,
And finish what we here began;
Heav'n will the mysteries explain,
And then, ah then, we'll understand.

Refrain

We'll know why clouds instead of sun
Were over many a cherished plan;
Why song has ceased when scarce begun;
'Tis there, some time, we'll understand.

Refrain

God knows the way, He holds the key,
He guides us with unerring hand;
Some time with tearless eyes we'll see;
Yes, there, up there, we'll understand.

Refrain

I've Overcome

You give me hope when I get weary,
you bring joy when the day is dreary
You say let's press on
even after the day's work is supposed to be done
Thank you for bringing laughter
to a child who has known only tears
proof that you have dealt with my worst fears
And today after the great farewell
You will stay with many sad stories to tell
Even if you weep as you sweep the floors
We know it's all in the game of opening doors
While others doze and nod
know that we are near to the heart of God
One day God will say "Well done"
And a child will exclaim "I've overcome."

(This is a poem I penned in 1996 at the children's home after the conclusion of the annual general meeting. I was encouraging staff to remain committed to the work of healing hurting lives in spite of it often being a thankless job.)

To my parents, John and Helen Gaffley; my wife, Desiree; our children, John, Michaela, Timothy, and Stephen; my brother Gerald; my sisters, Maureen, Jane, and Irene; and my mother-in-law, Magdalene Hendricks, who all helped to shape my identity and my reality. To God be the glory that He had a sense of humor with me.

Chapter One

My African Dream

Children are potent, recurrent and conflicting images in the human psyche, the repository of the traditional and the agents of social regeneration, little devils and trailers of divine glory, possessions and gifts, autonomous beings and newly fashioned retreads of their worn-out parents." We are both the continuation of previous generations and a unique expression of that continuity.

—William James (1842-1910)

What does it mean to be alive? What are you living for? What keeps you going? Are you grateful for your life? While many people may take life for granted, others are aware of the issues involved because of the daily friction that they have to endure. It is great to be alive and to live. Pain is a commonality in most of our lives. Pain conditions, shapes, defines, incapacitates, and handicaps many lives. However, pain can liberate, engineer change, and can energize. Pain whether physical, mental or emotional becomes almost unbearable when it is twinned with rejection. It is painful to live when you are ill-treated and marginalized because of the color of your skin. It is great to vote and to participate in democracy. It is painful to be politically disabled because of the color of your skin. Oppression means that access and opportunity are denied to those being discriminated against. Growing up in a political, social, and economic culture and climate that produced colored trucklers was frustrating, and survival was the only endeavor and immediate worry. In order to survive and to live in a color-biased context, you need courage, access to opportunity, and support. Life is what happens or the activity and actions that occur in the tension-filled moment between our memory of the past and our expectation for the future. Life is about what we are doing and being now. It is never easy to focus on who you are and what you do amid the many voices that want to inform you otherwise because an ideology that seeks to make you truckle. Sometimes the only strength that you have is the power of your mind. You are sometimes forced to allow the oppressor to shackle your physical movements, but you can never allow the oppressor to shackle your mind. We can so easily become classically conditioned to bow down and to serve the needs of the oppressor at the expense of our own unmet needs. We have to surpass what was physically done to us by enacting life, the present, between remembering and hope. The pendulum of life, although fixed in the moment, the present, is energized in the swing between past and present. Our memory is often the glue that keeps our lives coherent in spite of the physical pain. We engage life best by transcending our past in the actions we are taking with a firm view of future expectations or hope. Hope then becomes a joyous celebration of the unknown and an overcoming of the past. You have to focus on the harvest in spite of the painful toil in the moment.

I am a son of Mother Africa, the cradle of civilization. Africa, as its name indeed suggests, is the birthplace, the land free from cold and horror. I can recall only two significant natural disasters during my lifetime as a South African. I remember visiting with friends when an earthquake hit Ceres, South Africa, on September 29, 1969. On August 29, 1999, a tornado hit Cape Town on a Sunday morning. I mobilized a recovery team to help with the mop-up operation. This tornado hit some of the poorest areas of Cape Town. Many families of the children in residential care at the agency I was directing at the time were overcome by this disaster. Three people were killed.

Africans just love the sunny skies, *braaivleis* (barbecue), and long walks in the countryside. We will easily tell you that it is not far to go, when in fact it will be a few more miles before we reach our destination. Africa is the second largest continent. My dad told me about the preeminence of the African Dream long before I started reading about the American Dream. Africa is still a dream destination for aspiring international travelers. Africa is still my dream, my escape, and my refuge in a pristine environment surrounded by the sounds, sights, and aromas of Mother Nature.

When I became excited about Africa's greatness because the world's first heart transplant was performed at the Groote Schuur Hospital on December 3, 1967, my late father told me about Africa's former glory years. He told me about Africa's ancient kingdoms. He told me about Egypt and its kings and dynasties. He told me about Ethiopia, whose lines ran back to King Solomon and the queen of Sheba. He told me about Carthage (present-day Tunisia) being the capital of the Africa Province during Roman times. The Africa that I know is not comprised of mutually exclusive "tribal" nations. Trade missions and pacts existed in North Africa in spite of the absence of it in many written records. The existence of Mapungubwe as a trading post where Zimbabwe, Botswana, and South Africa meet is one such proof. Archaeological excavations have made discoveries about this metropolis that thrived from AD 1050 to AD 1270. Mapungubwe is regarded as South Africa's first kingdom.

Hollywood movies and the media still portray a much-skewed, negative, and maligned view of Africa. The people of Africa are often ridiculed. This continent is currently known for its human crises, problems, conflict, and the subsequent suffering of its peoples. It is known for famine caused by drought and other natural disasters. However, most of the harm done to

Africa has been done by people—people who were not born in Africa but who wanted what Africa had.

The West, notably the Europeans, brought the racism "plant" to Africa where it soon became naturalized and exploited in well-orchestrated social conditions. They sliced, diced, and divided Africa at will without ever consulting any African country, changing both the landscape and map of Africa to suit their exploits. In the international struggle for dominion over Africa, Europeans were besotted with the inferiority-superiority paradigm, and Africa has suffered much because of this implanted notion of the inferiority of the black peoples. The inferiority mantra gave Europeans a cover for exploiting Africa and its peoples, most notably the enslavement of Africans and the colonization of Africa. The second-class citizenship that they gave to the blacks gave them political power to dominate the majority. Their negative depiction of Africans duped the world into believing that Africans were primitive, barbaric savages. Africa was the continent that had to be saved, and Africans had to become civilized and regenerated. What a grand scheme to hide their greed and need for Africa's mineral wealth! They were not only interested in the mineral wealth of Africa, but also in its human capital. Hence a lucrative slave trade that ripped more than 20 million men from their families ensued. They would work on plantations and mines in the Americas and the Caribbean. Later the bulk of the slaves were needed for American plantation expansion and economic growth.

I have a notion that a lot of the medical and physical "findings" about nonwhites are not only skewed, but that society also continues to distort, demean, and depict people of color as different and inferior. Their physical features seem to be inferior. Their genes seem to be inferior. Their culture seems to be less civilized, their business acumen seems to be deficient, and their music seems to be inferior. The way they worship seems to be primitive, too noisy, and inferior. Their behavior in public is deemed to be undesirable, and they drive fear into people when they see people of color in groups. It sometimes appears that the darker the color, the more fear is invoked. Snide remarks are passed about them, and they are still ridiculed. Colored men are often deemed hectically macho and colored women too sexy for their station in life. When a colored person achieves greatness, it is a surprise. When they do well, it is as if society is relieved that they have managed to steer them away from prison.

People of color are ridiculed because they often have to make excuses. I agree that some of the excuses are lame, to say the least. The fine line between excuses and explanations are often missed. Excuses can at least explain why some of the behavior may seem to be so random. However, they can play the race card, the health card, the poverty card, or the overcrowding card. The fact is that some of the excuses are legitimate. Excuses like "My mom had lung cancer and my dad died of a heart attack" can be momentarily overwhelming. Excuses like "I could not do it because our electricity was cut and we had no money for food" can be embarrassing. "I am sorry for the inconvenience caused by my lateness but I had to take three buses to get here"; "I was absent yesterday because my brother-in-law in a drunken stupor beat the consciousness out of my sister the night before and I had to nurse and protect her"; "I am exhausted, overwhelmed, mentally and physically drained and I just cannot handle this stress anymore because life has just become too much"—these excuses often become labels for ordering and defining colored people.

May I respectfully remind the reader that these negative connotations originated in a time when racism was rife? They stem from a world order that had to prove that people were inferior or superior based on their skin color. Skin color has to do with who I am in the world of the ignorant, the people who do not know that it is what is inside of me that defines who I am. There is nothing wrong with my physical essence either, something that I cannot change because it is the extension of a union between my mom and dad.

We are now entering a time period when society is being forced by world events and movements to have real expectations for all people and not to lower their expectations just because of the color of a person's skin. I have always held the view that Africa should be allowed to do for Africa what Africa needs. The sooner Africa becomes less reliant on foreign aid, the better. The international world has meddled in Africa's affairs and has continued to muddy Africa's domestic or internal affairs. Africa will find solutions to Africa's problems. In any event, the aid that comes to Africa always has strings attached. Africa has great leaders who can deal with the not-so-great leaders. Why should Africa play second fiddle in solutions to its own problems? Foreign aid seems to complicate the solution process. The African learned helplessness has to end for the African renaissance to blossom.

I am proud to be who I am. I do not question my existence, I affirm it. I believe that I may have a predisposition to disease not because of the fact that I am black or a person of color but because of the multifarious struggles that I had to endure as a child and continue to carry with me in my imaginary bag filled with "survival powder," which every so often gets bumped into, and a puff of survival powder is manifest in my behavior. I am often confused about what is really happening. The first years of my life were just black and white—or were it white and black? What was was not really—or was it? Let me explain this aspect to you. I was taught to respect adults. That's the reality. However, another reality was seeing a white child disrespect my mom, and that was considered to be right. My mom allowed it, and this was the confusing, constant conflict.

I grew up in apartheid South Africa as a member of the so-called colored group, and for more than forty years, I was socialized by my family, my school, my church, my peers, and the political system. The political landscape of apartheid South Africa is almost impossible to explain, but an understanding of this issue is crucial to understanding the challenges I faced. In keeping with the history of Africa, the white minority had to find a way to keep the black majority in check in order for the whites to have political power. To this end, South Africa had a four-framed typology representation for its picture of race until 1994. In order to keep the divisions and reinforce a race-focused society, the white minority regime used the term *colored* to describe one of the four main typologies or racial groups identified by law: whites, Indians, coloreds, and blacks. Although the reference was to "biological" features, it impacted the social fabric. Whites were said to be superior to Indians, Indians were superior to coloreds, and coloreds superior to blacks. Although there was a closer alliance between whites and coloreds, the economic power of the Indians often relegated the position of coloreds.

Children grow up believing that life works the way their parents show them it does because they know of no other way yet. I have always had an uneasy feeling about life. I know that it is never easy to question the instruction and admonition of your parents. The first cracks in my perception about life appeared when I was issued a passport to visit Europe and America to attend a conference involving young people who had been marginalized and who were living in high-risk environments. The ultimate crack however was when I had to interact with my peers in Europe and America, and this forced me to revisit the repository of my childhood. I wrestled with the conflicting images in the nuanced, complicated reality of the apartheid era. My life view experienced an abrupt conversion in Europe when I was forced to negotiate my life without those apartheid direction signs that regulated access for whites and nonwhites. The conflict in my soul was painfully apparent. I did not know what to do until I entered into new mutually beneficial interpersonal relationships with people who were free from oppression. I was socialized to stand at the back of the line for most things. I was conditioned to stand at the back of the line and to wait for my turn to be announced by someone superior. Now I was invited to do a keynote speech, and it felt funny to be the focus of attention. Initially I was so excited to be talking that I hardly gave other people a chance to get their words in as well. I eventually assumed a position that would neither be up close and violating personal space nor aloof and withdrawn.

Once upon a life, things happen over which one has no control. When you do gain control, it is your duty to empower others to control their own destinies. I am now at the point where I want to let go of party politics and do what is right for my country and right for the world. I am struggling with this because I believed that I would vote for the ANC (African National Congress) forever. The current political situation in South Africa makes it complicated for me and others like me who want to help people to help themselves and to find at least some semblance of happiness on this earth in spite of their often overwhelming situations. I know that there are people who want to get involved and alleviate what others have to endure on a daily basis. They will, however, remain passive until a moment when something happens and they are compelled to make their presence count. They then move out of their comfort zones and join with others in a collective effort to make a difference.

The inauguration of Barack Obama as president of the United States of America is making people rethink and rework their stereotypes as well as their vocabulary. It is amazing how the word *mulatto* has become a popular term to use, especially for those who are uncomfortable to accept that a person other than white is in power. All of a sudden, a word that was demeaning in many cultures has become popular again. The world seems to still have a need to classify people in terms of their complexion. I salute whites in both South Africa and the United States who were brave enough to vote their conscience irrespective of the color of the candidates.

The birth of a worldview where the complexion of one's skin is no longer a preferential treatment passport is slowly shaping up, although older stereotypes are stubborn in shipping out. People of color are still deemed to be inferior because they are deemed to be different—inferior and different to whom and to what? Is there a genetic standard or measuring rod? I believe that studies that find that black and colored people have a greater predisposition to be infected by disease have to be revisited. However, this mind-set in the medical field is difficult to prove because it is largely anecdotal and is communicated via innuendo. It is often subtle, and in this area, older movies and documentaries do a great job of portraying this mind-set. Documentary evidence of the disparity in health insurance premiums based on race in the not-too-distant past is indisputable. People of color paid more for their health insurance than did whites. It is similar to the current practice where women pay more for their health insurance than men.

I believe that we should have the picture of people in totality. We come to the runway of life with our baggage. This baggage is weighing us down. This baggage is obliterating who we really are and can be. The baggage that white is deemed to be superior has created and conditioned many of our parents and relatives and friends. Studies have shown that even black children think that white dolls are superior and more beautiful. If you ask most people what the color of fairies are, they will say white, totally unaware that they have been classically conditioned through among others, the media. It is often awkward to think of fairies as being black. Oh sure, we can easily think of witches and wizards as being black. Does anyone have any idea of the impact of this baggage on the socialization of our children? Right now we would do well if we ensured that every child has at least one adult on whom he or she can depend for safety, shelter, support, and sustenance. There are a growing number of children from homes where fathers and mothers are absent and their communities are fragmented.

One thing that continues to amaze me is the denial in other sectors of a nation when another sector is being oppressed. I have spoken to both black and white adults in South Africa who were children at the same time I was, and they shared confusion similar to mine. I was especially surprised by white children who shared the fact that their moms were questioning what was happening, especially to black and colored children.

You have to remember that the police, who were so brutal, had families and had to go home and the saving grace for them that there was limited graphic material about the atrocities committed by them against blacks, coloreds, and Indians. Even when television was introduced in 1975, its broadcasts were still controlled by the state. We have not yet fully realized the role played by white women in bringing apartheid to an end. There are many stories about white women having sympathy with the plight of the oppressed. I have spoken to some of these women and know of the anguish that some of them felt at the time. Conversations were often uncomfortable for them. Their emotional conflict was often well masked to suit the company they were with or their comfort level to continue the conversation.

I need to survive at all costs. Stuff happens and we react from the wellspring of what has been accumulating within us since the day we were born. Our children in the former Group Areas Act, Act No. 41 of 1950 demarcated townships in South Africa, are often tired at birth and continue to grow up fatigued and sleepy. We are born numbed in our senses. I humbly submit that the children of color who grew up under the apartheid regime have a fair share of internal conflict. I am also convinced that white children were equally confused by what they saw and heard during the apartheid era.

In our household, we were taught to use the function of our olfactory nerve, but when we did and said that a white person's house was smelly, we would get a whack against the head. I remember visiting the house of very wealthy people that my late mom used to work for. When they opened the front door, I immediately pulled on my mom's dress and tried to whisper loudly that their house was stinking because I thought that I was making a great discovery. So this *should I*, *should I not*, *is it*, *is it not* struggle continued in our innermost beings. People often cannot understand why people of color react the way they do. The intertwining of the consequences of poverty and race were the prongs that pinned me down. These consequences were neither logical nor natural. It was confusing, and it felt as if my life was in a grip that was hard to overcome. However, neither poverty nor race ultimately defined me. I became who I am not because of apartheid, but in spite of it. I wish I could say to you that color does not matter in the United States, but it does—and it is still causing conflict. However, there is a subtle difference: in the United States, a person of color can be accepted and treated essentially the same with the right amount of money, education, celebrity, or other forms of status.

So much has changed South Africa, yet so much remains the same. In spite of the so-called nonracial manifesto of the ruling party, I still have to define who I am. My horizon has not yet broadened. I still visit the same places, worship in the same church, and have the same friends and family. I am still a person of color. In America, I am just a South African. I go where I want, worship where I want, and associate with whom I want. Color does not matter because I am educated and I can pay my way.

Color is definitely not part of the referencing grid in the language or mind-set of my children, and I am happy for this generational gap. I have overcome, and they do not even know what it is that I overcame. My children are growing up "color-blind," and they continue to respect people irrespective of the color of their skin. My friends were chosen for me by color. I was told that I could not play with, nor interact with, children of colors other than mine. I had to work and renegotiate my way out of the color-coding blinkers. I had to go for counseling to amend this defective mind-set. There comes a point when we all have to let go and let God, and when we have to embrace the new reality that will hopefully not be as conflicted as the former.

My wife, our children, and I are just so thrilled and honored to be living in America and to witness a radical change in politics for the second time. In 1994, the Republic of South Africa elected its first black president, Nelson Rolihlahla Mandela, and initiated the transformation from apartheid to democracy and a human rights culture for all. Nelson Mandela had a vision of a free and democratic society and was prepared to die for it. He lived to usher in a human rights culture that will evolve, for a human rights culture is a journey, not the attainment of a milestone.

In 2009, the United States of America inaugurated its first black president, Barack Hussein Obama. America has embarked on a journey unlike any other before. The stereotypes will have to change, and the historical models will not serve this generation and its challenges well, if at all. In South Africa, we could not use the historical models because that would be tantamount to idolizing our oppressors. How America will redefine history will be a complex activity. How blacks and whites will redefine their history and their lives as Americans will be interesting to behold. One thing that I know is that the blacks will become much more confident about who they are. No doubt, President and Mrs. Obama will pave the way for a new presidential culture, new icons, new jokes, new songs and lyrics, new paradigms, new fashions, and new government departments and buildings. Many people will want to emulate his superb organization and oratory skills. Let the record stand that he ran an impressive presidential election campaign.

The current economic crisis required the new president to hit the ground with his taskforce, toolkit, and trademark tenacity on January 20, 2009. The tanking economy, however, may be in some ways a veiled blessing, in that it will keep America focused on the priorities of rebuilding national pride and it will prevent Americans from wasting their energy on petty party political squabbles, innuendo, and pointless political pandering. In my humble opinion, America will be wise to know that this election does not undo the suffering and exploitation of black people over many, many years. Among the whites, there will no doubt be a few diehards who find the election of a black as president deplorable. The de facto divisions caused by poverty in the country will have to be addressed, wisely, because my chief concern is what difference it will make in the lives of developing children. It is this generation of children that will have to extend America into the future as a global power of repute or of disrepute. I have travelled around the world and seen the poverty pockets. The consequences of poverty and its impact on children is the same the world over. Poor children look similar. Poverty is confusing and often defies logic. As a child growing up in apartheid South Africa, I could never understand why life looked so free and easy for supporters of the regime. However, for us who lived in our wood and iron dwellings, our posies, our shacks, it was sometimes fun and sometimes painful. Our houses were always overcrowded, yet there was always a place for more strangers and families to join us. This is a great time to consider the values we teach all our children and to move children's issues to the top of our political agendas. I believe that any nation that is serious about patriotism, national security, the economy, and the future has to take its investment in its children seriously. If you do not value your children, you have no right to the future. We know from research that 85 percent of a child's intellect and personality is formed by age five. Current research findings demonstrate that well-designed early childhood settings that promote healthy development and stimulate early learning help children achieve in school and in life, with particularly dramatic positive impacts on disadvantaged children. Nobel Laureate James Heckman, an economist at the University of Chicago, states that investments in high-quality early education programs are cost effective, with the highest rate of return of any social investment. In spite of the current economic situation, the question is not whether we can afford to invest in our children and youth but rather can we afford not to invest in them if they are the future of any nation.

Sekunjalo! Life is what it is; let it flow don't dam it, don't damn it. What are you living for? Life is most meaningful when the pain of striving for change is less than the pain of staying the same. Be the blessing you want. Be and receive a blessing. Do not let the halo of your professional arrogance dim the relevance of your humaneness.

Your attitude mirrors your thoughts. Value others as you would that they value you. Stop blaming others. Blaming others robs you of energy: eventually you will be absent in your presence, fatigued by your own devices and constant defeats. Celebrate the gift of life, joyfully, moment by moment. Appreciate the simple things, even the seemingly insignificant. See beyond the present sweat and toil as you sow, anticipating the harvest. Thankfulness fortifies effort, boosts performance, and fuels your courage to survive. What is done or not done is done, sometimes. Cocreate a milieu worth living in for all.

Leaving a legacy is essence, not appendage, to doing Life 101. I see my life as a gift. I have not earned it nor do I necessarily deserve it. I understand my role as a teacher. We are all teachers who never stop teaching. Someone is always watching our example, even when we think no one is watching. I want to help children, young people, and peers to develop a love for learning. I have learned not to judge others, because as long as I am critical of them, they cannot be my teachers and I cannot learn from them. I do not give up on a challenge. I always said to the abused children, when they were acting out in the residential care center where I worked, that no matter how bad they behaved, I would not give up and that I would not be the one whose back they can point to as another one who walked away from them. I always believed that I do not have the power to change my customers, clients, students, and friends because only they have the power to change, if they want to and when they have to. Just as you cannot make a baby sleep, you cannot force people to embrace change. People do not resist embracing change, they resist being changed. I believe that anger complicates the search for a solution and that revenge makes the wound worse. I believe that hatred eventually destroys your life and that forgiveness sustains a worthwhile life. I believe that you cannot release your capability and capacity to love unless you set the pain in your life free.

I have learned the art and science of exploratory cocreative dialogue. I listen. I feel. I let it flow. I believe, I trust, I make myself vulnerable to be disappointed. I believe in a higher order that has the last word.

Looking back over my life, I see oppression in the distance, yet there is propinquity between my past and my present. The fusion of past and present is often exacerbated by pain. I see the scars on my body and visualize painful memories of a time when I was the vulnerable victim. My life was a shattered, fragmented mess. I was an angry, very bitter young man who would not let a fly rest on my nose without a violent reaction.

In this moment and in the future, I see opportunities to connect and make a difference. I am a victor. I have a message. I am better and no longer bitter and angry. I am a survivor. I have obtained an education in order to serve people and to never look down on others. I have overcome brutality and violence. I am a winner. I am not all that I ought to be; I still have many, many imperfections. I am not all that I want to be; I still have many aspirations. I am not all that I am supposed to be, but I thank God that I am not what I used to be.

My personal vision statement: *Deo Servire Vera Libertas*, which means "Freedom through Service to God."

I am referring to this publication as *Flatline to Change*. A flatline or inactivity on either an electrocardiogram or an electroencephalogram signifies death. My flatline arrived unannounced, and for me, a flatline is the opposite of change because a flatline is even direr than the maintenance of the status quo. A flatline is indicative of no energy, no movement, no pulse, no blood flow, no heartbeat, and an absence of resilience. A flatline is tantamount to being rigor mortis, rigid.

On Saturday, February 16, 2008, I suffered a severe heart attack in Fort Lauderdale, Florida, USA. I had to be resuscitated twice—first with 120 electric volts and then with 150 volts. This book is about what happened in the fleeting moment when I was "dead." My life just flashed by. I saw all the conflicting images of my childhood. Although absent in this moment, I was very present in that moment. Everything was structured, sequenced, and live. I was in a moment where my childhood and adulthood experiences were coeval.

Let me back up just a bit. First, there was a bright white screen like the start of a movie. First, the words of hymns that I like to recite while on the treadmill came on the "screen," and then as if in a giant theater, the images of my childhood started rolling, slowly at first, and then increasing in frequency and intensity. Now that I am writing this account, it is as if I was reinterpreting my life and what happened in reality and in this near-death experience.

In retrospect, it was as if I was looking in a giant rearview mirror. It was as if there was a seamless connection between what flashed by and with what I was. There was a kind of paradoxical integration between being and doing. I still cannot fully explain that moment. I relived a lifetime. No, I relived a lifestyle as a voiceless, invisible participant. Since that moment, I have had an expanded understanding of the reality of my childhood events and traumatic experiences. This flashback is fueling my courage to change my life and to reach out to others who may also want to change their lives. I want to touch the lives of children and especially young people.

I want to connect with them when they cry alone. I want to connect with them when they are perplexed. I want to connect with them when they create a danger to others while trying to create a safe space for themselves. I want to connect with them as they build their career with minimal resources. I want to connect with them when they are disappointed and made to feel rejected. I want to connect with them when they consider suicide. I want to connect with them because although their electrical time sequence measurement indicates activity and they may in fact be busy and active, their flatline is the result of a complete breakdown of their relationships and everything that gives meaning to their lives. Mark Barton, Seung-Hui Cho, Robert Hawkins, Joseph Pallipurath, Terry Ratzmann, Norman Afzal Simons, Robert Stewart, Bryan Uyesugi, and Jeff Weise are not just names. These are the names of people whose flatline produced a flatline tragedy that devastated neighborhoods. We need to act fast in order to avert a repeat of these kind of preventable tragedies. Many of these people were disconnected from their neighborhood of origin. There was pain. The pain was unattended. The pain generated more pain. When will we debunk the myth that time heals or that time is a healer? Time in these instances was the producer of a tragic event. Each one's pain crafted and directed a plan that was enacted over time and suddenly the neighborhood realized that it ran out of time to identify and respond to flatline people. I will discuss flatline people and neighborhoods later on in this book.

They may in fact be living, yet dead because their social network provides neither support nor stimulus. If life has no joy and nothing makes you happy and nothing you do makes a meaningful difference, what are you living for? They may just be breathing and no longer seeing the beauty of the sky, the stars, the trees, the ocean, and the birds. They may no longer hear the beauty in the laughter and chatter of small children. They may no longer hear the urgency in a baby's cry because they were abandoned and left crying. They may no longer smell the scent of roses and stare at butterflies in the garden. The perpetual motion of unrequited love and romance can frustrate them. They may become desperate, and there is no telling what a desperate person will do when cornered. The extremity of pain that children and young people experience may not be caused directly by the adults in their primary environment, but adults can always make a difference to the flatline in at least one child's life. Alternatively, the adult weariness in the lives of children and young people will just become more manifest in the behavior of these disappointed children and young people as they grow older.

On Sunday, February 3, I went to Cleveland, Ohio, for a weeklong board meeting at Saw Mill Creek Resort, a beautiful 235-acre facility on Lake Erie between Toledo and Cleveland. The Friday before I left for Ohio, I received the results of some recent blood work, and for the first time, my cholesterol level was down. I was elated. The medical profession always reminds me that my high cholesterol is a genetic gift and that high cholesterol runs in my family.

Every morning while I was in Ohio, I would run on the treadmill for an hour from six until seven. One colleague and I were about the only people in the gym at that time. I did the treadmill until the Thursday when I left to come home to Fort Lauderdale. On Friday, I went to my office on the university campus where I have a full-time faculty position.

On Saturday, February 16, I got up early, went to the grocery store to get some fresh breakfast goodies, returned and made my wife breakfast in bed. While she was having her breakfast, I took our son Timothy to his weekend job at Warrick's Hobby Store on University Drive in Plantation, Florida. My wife eventually left to attend a Saturday women's group at church about half a mile away to the northwest from our house. My youngest son, Stephen, and I were home alone. My eldest son, John, was away at work on a yacht in St. Thomas. My daughter Michaela, a student, was at the campus of the University of Miami.

I went outside to mow the grass. It was hot outside. Wow! My vision became blurry. I felt faint and sweaty. I tried to make my way inside to get some water. I could not see the refrigerator. I asked my son to pass me some water. He thought that I was joking. Eventually he gave me the water. I drank it. My vision was restored after about one minute. The faintness dissipated. I decided not to go back outside in the heat.

Instead, I continued with the remodeling of the children's bathroom. I had taken out the damaged bathtub the night before and had replaced the inside walls. I struggled, lying over the side of the bathtub for about an hour to line up the hole in the bathtub with the waste connector in the ground. Once the bathtub was aligned and installed, I started to tile the walls. Tiling is what I did until about 5:00 p.m. when my wife, Desiree, reminded me that we were going to dinner with our daughter. Being male, I would usually react with a can't-you-see-that-I-am-almost-done attitude. But no, I immediately packed up, cleaned the tools, and packed the stuff away in the garage. I then went to take a shower in the master bedroom shower. The strange thing is that I remember not locking the bathroom door, and I usually do. I showered, stepped out of the shower, whistled, and bent down to dry my feet. Wow! I had a sharp pain in my chest. I struggled to stand up straight. I made my way to the bedroom and asked my wife to please put on my socks while I was holding my chest. My wife referred to me as grandpa while she was putting on my socks and pants.

Once dressed, I made my way to the car, a silver Chevrolet Malibu. Once outside, the pain was just unbearable. It felt as if the excruciating pain was dripping from my body. Again, the male in me wanted to be macho and "wise." However, pain is a director. Pain directed me to the hospital. I told Michaela, my son Stephen, and Katie, Michaela's friend, to go for dinner in the Dodge Caravan while Timothy, my son, would take me to the hospital with my wife. Just before we reached the 441 off-ramp on the I-595 travelling east on our way to the Broward General Hospital, I asked Timothy for a bottle of water to ease the pain, which I thought and secretly hoped was just indigestion. The water was magic. The pain was gone. The absence of pain made me give a directive to join Michaela at the restaurant. My wife and kids were confused and dumb with silence. I could see the agony etched on their faces. Oh how it must have felt like a sword ripping through their hearts. They were very nervous and tried not to do or say anything that might upset me.

Whoa! When we arrived in the parking bay of the restaurant, the pain reemerged, only ten times worse than before. I could hardly stand. It felt as if I was going to lose bowel and bladder control. I begged to be taken to the hospital, which was mercifully a few blocks away from the restaurant. Timothy weaved through the traffic like a Mario Andretti while I just about bent or broke the headrest on the passenger side front seat. I begged him to go faster. I was crying and being brave. I was in pain but wanted to stay in control. I started thinking that I was not going to make it without wetting and/or soiling myself.

When we arrived in the emergency section of Memorial Pembroke Regional Hospital on Sheridan Street, my blood pressure was 116/72, and the one nurse told me to sit and wait my turn while the other disagreed and took me into the emergency room. The last thing that I remember was lying down on a gurney in the aisle. I passed out. My heart stopped. I stopped breathing. I died. During this time I had this near-death experience. This is the time when I had the flashbacks. This is the time when being spectator and participant of the events and encounters of my life were coeval.

I awoke on a bed in another room, and it seemed as if the doctor and nurses were rather happy. I was asked my name and my social security number. I knew both. I was told that I was going to be taken to another hospital for a procedure. I could not understand the smile of relief on the face of the medics in the room.

With sirens wailing, I was rushed to another hospital, Memorial West Hospital on Flamingo Road. They did not even put my shirt back on or close me with a blanket. The two medics in the ambulance kept talking to me and asking me questions. They warned that I should not fall asleep. The surprising fact is that we live less than a mile from the fire station, and I never paid attention to the wailing of the sirens. Now, however, I bet I hear the wailing of every fire engine that is being dispatched day or night. Now I just say a prayer that they will be in time to prevent a flatline and to reduce the suffering of someone.

I know nothing about what happened at Memorial West until I woke up in the Intensive Care Unit at about ten thirty the evening. I was told by the cardiologist that they had to put a stent into the left anterior descending artery of my heart because it was 100 percent occluded. He told me that I had suffered a cardiac arrest and that the extent of the myocardial infarction was not yet known. He told me that they had to resuscitate me twice and that I was a miracle because there were no scorch marks on my chest.

At about eleven, one of the nurses moved me (which she was instructed not to do), and the catheter inserted into my groin came out. They tried for more than an hour to stop the bleeding. One doctor stood for an hour with his hand firmly on my groin. My blood pressure continued to drop. In my sort of delirious state, I heard the nurse say that she knows that I am a believer and that she will sing hymns to me. At about four thirty that morning, I finally fell asleep. I stayed in the ICU for four days and was discharged. John arrived from St. Thomas. I had many visitors from the church and university. I had a relapse on March 3 and landed back in the hospital in Aventura. They just pumped me full of chemicals. They were planning to do test after test. I insisted to be discharged into the care of my cardiologist.

I would still not have written this account until I received the latest findings of my blood works a week ago. It simply stated that my cholesterol was down to the under-200 mark but that my triglycerides was spiking at over 300. They told me that triglycerides usually go up when your cholesterol goes up and when your weight increases. Well, in my case, my weight was down by 35 pounds, and my cholesterol was down by 44 points. I was sticking to my heart healthy diet and my daily exercise. Was something else at play here?

Well, when I had that heart attack, my powder bag was opened, emptied and hopefully thrown away. I will for the next three months not change my eating pattern, my medication, or my lifestyle. I believe that this book is my therapy.

This then is the musings that spawned the conception of this book. Let me then invite you to the concert of my life. Unfortunately, I cannot give you a program of my life because the program can only be printed after my earthly sojourn is over. When we enter the stage of this world's theater at birth, not even our parents as our personal ushers can give us the program detailing future events, crises, and opportunities, for the outcome of even their intervention in our lives are unpredictable. Life or our personal program is the narrative of what really happens after and in spite of the challenges we encounter.

Remember that we are living in a world that has been turned upside down by the current economic crisis. No one person or nation has what it takes to fix our world. We can only hope that a collective effort by world leaders will minimize the suffering and promote a benign recovery.

Chapter Two

Lifestyle Challenges

> *When we least expect it, life sets us a challenge to test our courage and willingness to change; at such a moment, there is no point in pretending that nothing has happened or in saying that we are not ready. The challenge will not wait.*
>
> —Paulo Coelho (1947-)

I was born on a Tuesday, the 153rd day of the year. I was raised in Cape Town, South Africa. I am a Gemini. I am an ENTP on the Myers-Briggs Personality Test. I am a reformed protestant in the Calvinist tradition. I love sports, not as a spectator but as a participant. I have been married to the same delightful wife for thirty years. We have three handsome sons and one beautiful daughter. Our current dog's name is Louie.

On the same day that Queen Elizabeth II of England took the Coronation Oath of Office in Westminster Abbey on June 2, 1953, in front of eight thousand dignitaries, I was born in a simple wood and iron dwelling to John and Helen Gaffley (nee Langtry) at 190 De Villiers Street, Vasco. My parents were the products of biracial marriages. I was in grade one when I first realized that I was born into the so-called Cape colored group and that I had inherited all the blessings associated with members of this group. As far as my mom could recall, I suffered no prenatal, peri-natal, or postnatal stress. I was the last of six children. I had four sisters and a brother. My eldest sister died at age six. My second eldest sister died at age fifty-five. We lived in a pink house. When it rained, we had to move pots and buckets around on our beds and the floor to catch the water that leaked in through the roof. I just loved rainy days because it was not a usual day. The house was warm, cozy, and homely. We kept the house warm in winter by making a fire outside in paraffin tins and then we would bring in the coals. We would also roast peanuts and candy over these coals. We were never allowed to shoot firecrackers because my family reminded us about Guy Fawkes and his plot. Fireworks were associated with this, and in many Commonwealth countries, Bonfire Night was observed on November 15.

Although our house was built from wood and iron, we never had to worry that our house would be blown away by tornadoes, hurricanes, and other storms because Cape Town had a very mild Mediterranean climate. We had a variety of fruit trees and a beautiful vegetable and flower garden. In front of the house was a tall tree with a swing on which we played every day after school.

I was a product of the children of poverty. My parents were poor. We were all disadvantaged by the apartheid system because of the color of our skin. It was indeed complex to understand what was happening because of apartheid and poverty and what was happening because of a lack of parent training and education. It looked as if our parents were lacking in job skills, but job reservation for whites was the real reason for their difficulty in finding employment, even at the lowest rung of the employment ladder.

People think that the baby of the family is spoiled by parents and siblings. NO! Not true! Parent fatigue and the familiarity of child rearing disengages parents and puts siblings in charge of "the baby" because the baby is left with them when the parents have to run errands or respond to other demands of everyday life. I was unhappy but never really cried. It is awkward to be the sixth child. I always felt like a replacement for something. Only later on did I learn that my oldest sister, Yvonne, passed away at age six. There are many pictures of my siblings when they were small, but none of me. This was confusing to me, but I later realized that the novelty of a sixth child just did not warrant more family photo sessions.

I remember that I had to do a test in order to be allowed to attend first grade, then called Sub A, at Vasco North Primary School. I had to stand on my left leg, put my right arm over my head, and touch my ear. Should I be able to touch my ear, I was "ready for school." Only much, much later did I read about an anthropologist's stupid theory that the brains of black and colored people are smaller than those of whites. There was no kindergarten or reception grade prior to attending first grade at the primary school which was grade one to grade seven. Grades eight to twelve were high school, and then you attended university. Should you not have a matriculation exemption, you could attend technical college.

I remember being always willing to help others. At a very early age, I worked sorting fruit and vegetables, cleaning horse stables, burying the contents of chamber pots and the outside toilet, and cleaning the backyard. I sold newspapers on street corners shouting "*Argus, Argus,* today's newspaper, today." All the children had chores to do but it just seemed that mine were the dirtiest, crummiest chores. When I arrived home, we could all eat, and there was joy. We would cut up the partly bruised pieces from the fruit and put the healthy part in a huge enamel bowl. We called this "dessert of the angels," and it was the best dessert ever. I polished wooden floors on my knees at fifteen cents per room. My grandmother crocheted doilies, and I sold them to teachers at school by offering them the deal of paying it in two parts, one-half this month and the other the next. My mom embroidered aprons and made dresses, and I sold these during my childhood. Life was hard for me, but at twenty-one, I bought my first home, a beachfront property, with the money I had started saving at this early age.

I often wondered why there was so much pain in my life. I often wondered why I was surrounded by so much pain. I often wondered why life hurt so much. In my heart, I secretly asked God where he was, and if he was there, why was he so silent? I wondered whether he could see the injustices and the suffering of inflicted by the whites on people of color. I felt like Paul said in the Bible: "We are hard pressed on every side, but not crushed; perplexed, but not in despair, persecuted, but not abandoned; struck down but not destroyed" (2 Corinthians 4:8-9). It was as if I did not fit. I was uncomfortable. However, I could always repeat the entire church service and knew the words of most hymns by heart. Even church added to my conflict because I knew about the difficult lives some of the people in church were leading, yet they had the largest smiles and seemed to be so content in church. We were going to church, yet our conditions looked no better or different from that of our equally poor neighbors who did not attend church. I kept searching for this God that they say will provide for all our needs. In my heart and mind, the constant conflict raged about why I was smart and poor, why there was so much alcohol abuse and not enough food to eat. I guess that that is why I was always happy to be working and to block out time and opportunity to ask questions. I was always asked to do odd jobs for people in the neighborhood both in Vasco and in Kensington. I loved gardening and flying kites. I hated painting and the smell of paint. My only toy that I remember having was the lid of a saucepan, which was my imaginary car, and wherever I went, I would drive this lid. It was my transitional object.

I got my first long pants when I was in grade eight. I used to be donkey boy, which means that I carried the extra bag for the mailman around Christmastime. I always worked with the postman Harry DuPreez in Walmer Estate, District Six, and this money afforded me my first long pants. I was troubled. The emotional conflict caused by conflicting images and experiences made me uncomfortable. The more I did the right thing, the more my parents left me on my own. They were quick to respond to any trouble as it emerged in the lives of my siblings. I never understood why they did not understand my unhappiness with the situation that my parents let me face challenges as well as achievements on my own while my parents were paying attention to trouble caused by my siblings.

With all the violence, conflict, and abuse around me, I always had a sense that I was maybe not my parents' child because I could do nothing right and was blamed for everything that went wrong. My middle sister often shielded me from many unnecessary hiding. In South Africa, corporal punishment was the norm. Parents would often lash out with their hands, and the saying was that their hand of wisdom would connect with our seat of wisdom—meaning our heads.

I was in constant crisis. I did not know who I was. Society did not tell me who I was, my parents thought that I was difficult, and my loneliness continued until an event that affirmed this identity issue for me. One of the sons of my fourth-grade teacher was in class with me. He and I were always locked in our own duel for best academic performance. We had a science project, and his dad rated my project the best in class. He was emotionally upset by this and, in my presence, challenged his dad's assessment of the work done. To make matters worse for him, I won a national slogan writing competition for aspirin a few weeks later. I was elated, and from that day, I was not just a poor, lonely kid; I realized that what I had inside of me surpassed the shade on the outside. I embarked on a journey to get my inside outside.

I guess I wanted to be the perfect child and tried to perform and excel by becoming head boy of the school, winning *Eisteddfods*, which were districtwide and statewide arts and sciences competitions, math Olympiads, and other meritorious awards and scholarships. At nine years of age, I sang "Ave Maria" in the city hall in Cape Town. That night I will not forget! It was prestigious to sing in the city hall, but my mother sent my brother to go with me. He lost my jacket and I got a spanking. I continued to receive meritorious awards.

My mom and dad moved the family to Kensington in Maitland Estate, a suburb of Cape Town, in 1962 when I was nine years old. My dad had been transferred there to pastor the mother church of our denomination. This church housed the first medical clinic, welfare office, and primary school in this area. It served mainly coloreds and blacks. This church was a breakaway church from the then Dutch Reformed Church. The Dutch Reformed Church supported apartheid, and my grandfather did not support apartheid. My dad's father was a missionary who came from Belfast in Ireland. My mom's dad, Frank, and his brother William came to South Africa as WWI soldiers in 1914. They were Scottish, from Edinburgh.

I was introduced to electricity for the first time in this house. No more polishing of floors on my knees because that is why God and Columbus invented electric polishers. No more boiling water in a paraffin tin once a week for a warm bath. No more chopping wood in the forest in the afternoon. No more struggling to light the Welcome Dover stove with wet wood. We now had a refrigerator, electric stove, an electric iron, and a telephone. We had a hi-fi radiogram with reel-to-reel tape deck. We could play vinyl LPs and seven-inch singles. No longer did we have to wind up the gramophone and continuously check on the needle and the speed. Oh, the pure luxury of an indoor water closet (toilet) and a bath with running hot water! No more lighting of candles and lamps. No more struggling to do homework by candlelight.

One of the many memorable things that happened in Kensington when we had just moved in was that my youngest sister and I were teasing my grandfather. He got annoyed and threw a small pepper pot at us, which crashed into the glass of the kitchen dresser. My sister and I wrote a letter of apology to my mom, begging her forgiveness and promising to repay the damage by going to work for Mr. Davids, the shopkeeper of the corner store. We then went on our knees and prayed to God that my mom would not give us the hiding we deserved. We did not get a hiding because mom found us kneeling in front of her bed, fast asleep. Later, when we were teenagers, we would party together. Our favorite stomping ground was Worcester. We had a curfew of 10:00 p.m. When we were late, we had to find a good excuse or else we would get it good and solid. I remember one night we came in late and would surely get a hiding. However, when we knocked on the door and Mom came to the door with a cane, I remembered that we were celebrating Holy Communion in church the next morning. I then asked Mom why she was coming to us her children with a stick as if we were robbers and thieves and would she have the right frame of mind and heart to sit down at the Communion table with a clear conscience before God. You guessed it, it worked. We did not get a spanking . . . that time.

My dad was senior pastor of a church that did not pay him enough money to raise a family of five, and I always felt that we, the children, were paying for my dad's commitment and passion. I had great reservations about going into the pastorate and having to let my children pay or suffer for my commitment. He would typically be paid on the first Saturday of the month, typically the net proceeds of the collections and offerings on that day. Hence, we only ate dessert once a month, on the first Sunday following the first Saturday of the month, and we went on vacation the first four Sundays of January of every year, when we would all get into first his Ford Taurus station wagon, and then later his Peugeot, to go visit friends and family in rural areas. This ride was a mess because there was always fighting and bickering from the back because the ones in the back were fighting the ones in the front, pulling their ear, tugging their hair because none of us wanted to be in the car. And then, when we arrived at our destinations, we were told that this was Aunty So-and-So and Uncle So-and-So. We could never see the connection of how they were related to us—some of them were reeking of alcohol—but because they were aunty and uncle, we had to kiss them on the mouth as a sign of affection. Sometimes I felt like vomiting and would get in trouble for my refusal to kiss. Only much later did I realize that in our culture, everyone that connects with our living space, our most intimate environment, is family. This definition takes care of the complication of having to define and classify a mother, her boyfriend, and her daughter from another relationship.

When I was six years old, I went with my mom to visit my dad's cousin in Cape Town in Stuckeris Street. I had on a brown short pants and yellow cable patterned jersey. Stuckeris Street was adjacent to the big fruit and vegetable market. On this site today is the Good Hope Center. This was then the heart of District Six. District Six was an area that suffered under the Group Areas Act. The government expropriated the land for the exclusive use of white people. They moved the inhabitants of District Six to Bonteheuwel and other townships that were newly created on the Cape Flats, a former wasteland and wetland. The houses in Bonteheuwel were basically concrete cubes. Many people that were moved or relocated to Bonteheuwel suffered all sorts of diseases like tuberculosis and other chest and lung ailments. My dad didn't really want my mom to go because she had to be in church that evening, and if she went to District Six, she would not be in time for church. I remember my mom had on a floral dress that was buttoned down the middle. And I had just about broken off every button of that dress in pestering her for an ice cream. I heard the bell of the ice cream man and ran out to the balcony on the first floor. The balcony gave way, and I landed on my head in Stuckeris Street unconscious. I was rushed to Woodstock Hospital. My mom was frantic because on the one hand she feared the worst, and on the other, she feared my dad and what he was going to say if something happened to me while she was defying his direct instruction not to go to District Six. However, after eight hours unconscious, I came to and we went home and I wish I could say we lived happily ever after, but no. The next Saturday, I had on the same brown pants and yellow cable patterned jersey, my Sunday clothes. We were at the graveyard and my dad was holding my hand. I remember that without him noticing, I had dislodged the grasp of his hand and dashed across the street, and two cars going in opposite directions almost knocked into me. The result was I was standing in the middle of two cars going in opposite directions, and because each wanted to give way from each other, they gave way into each other. But, hey, I survived because I'm here today telling my story.

At one time, the church was organizing a picnic to Witsand (white sands), a beach on the east coast of South Africa. Now you must remember that the best beaches were reserved for whites, and if colored people wanted to go to the beach, they had to go to distant beaches. This would definitely be the rockiest and most uninhabitable beach space, with strong cross currents and lots and lots of seaweed. These were the beaches reserved for colored people. I cannot ever remember seeing black people on the beaches that we visited when I was a child. At this beach, Mom sent me to the tent of a fellow camper who came with us on the truck. Now a tent for me was just a blanket tied to trees like a shade cloth because colored people had no tents. And I, without her watching, walked in the wrong direction and kept on walking and could not find my way back; I was lost. And just before nightfall, they found me on a deserted beach, and I got the hiding of my life. I was just ten years old. I am the first and only one of the children of both my mom and dad's brothers' and sisters' children to have a university degree. I have about fifty first cousins.

I was always unhappy in church. The only times that I was happy was when my friends and I had to clean the school classrooms every day after school. We attended Sunday school on a Sunday afternoon at three o'clock. Like clockwork, the superintendent would put a peg (a clothespin) on my ear as a reminder to listen and to behave. I guess that I had reservations about my faith. This changed during the last year of high school when my dad sat me down and explained that faith does not make you a sissy and that faith does not obliterate your personality; it completes and perfects your personality. I used to sing in the church choir and was an active member of the youth organizations. I used to show movie films on a 16mm movie projector in the church hall to raise funds for the church. The movie was always well attended.

This was a great community church. We used to have lots of children's festivals and sporting concerts. They would sing all the old songs, folk songs, and war songs. One of the songs that I remember best is "If I Knew You Were Coming I'd Have Baked a Cake." In our church, there was a black guy and he was an elder. Abel Mokitimi was married to a colored woman named Frances. He was a tap dancer, and he was the nicest, friendliest gentleman I have ever known. He always used to whistle merry tunes. He was very generous in his praise of other people. He was very hygienic. I cannot ever remember him being sick. He was a panel beater (body work for cars) by trade, and the strange thing is that his children were basically named after children in my family. Abel Mokitimi was my trainer in chief and taught me about Nelson Mandela and the then banned African National Congress (ANC). He also made me aware of Steve Biko the Black Consciousness Movement leader who was basically and brutally murdered by the regime. How many other people Abel educated I'm not sure because I never ever heard anybody else talk about the ANC but him. We were told never to smile with a black person because if they see our teeth, they'll steal it. Abel Mokitimi lived in NY 56 in Guguletu (*NY* means "Native Yard") and access to this neighborhood was only through a police gate because the whole place was fenced in. Abel was a remnant of the black people living in Windermere, which was adjacent to Kensington. He lived in Macheko's block and another family that was black that I remember was the woman who sold the water on a horse and cart. Her name was Sicona. The blacks were all moved out of Windermere and relocated to Guguletu. Windermere became nonexistent and wiped off the map. The whites were redesigning the landscape as well as the maps at will, with no regard to the dignity of, and respect for, life. It was very common to see the landscape changing. Where once there were shanties (crudely built huts), there would be vacant land. Vast tracts of land would be reclaimed for weeds as the regime weeded out the legitimate inhabitants just because of the color of their skin. During the 1976 riots, we were told that Abel was sick and that is why he could not come to church. I remember one Sunday after church accompanied by my wife, we went to go and see Abel and his family. We were allowed into the compound because I was *umfundis* (clergy) and we took food with us, and to our horror and dismay, we discovered that they were just being cut off from the rest of the world and that he was not sick. A lot of these things are unknown to South Africans because we had no television and most of the press could not be anything other than progovernment. Television was only introduced into South Africa in 1975 for one hour a day. Guguletu is the same place where Amy Biel, an American Fulbright scholar committed to social justice, was slain on August 25, 1993. I remember this day because it was the same day that the guy who used to put a peg on my ear in Sunday school had his birthday.

During primary school, our games were mainly board games like draughts (similar to checkers) and Snakes and Ladders (known in the United States as Chutes and Ladders). Outside we played hopscotch, five stones where you would toss the stones and pick them up; Wolf, Wolf How Late Is It; and hide-and-seek. Girls played with their dolls, and boys played cowboys and crooks. We would spin tops and play with our marbles. Girls and boys always played separately. I was Prince Charming in the operetta *Snow White and the Seven Dwarfs*. The girls playing the part of Snow White and one of the fairies were my first introduction to girlfriends in grade seven, the end of primary school.

During high school, we played cannon, where you would place a piece of wood horizontally over a hole in the ground. With another piece of wood that you hold vertically, you would try and scoop up the piece of wood over the hole in the ground. The object was to try and see how far you could toss it. We played card games. Sometimes we played for money. A condom was called an FL ("French letter," meaning it should not be announced in public), and these were mainly used as water cannons. We played games in the street after school. We mainly played cricket and soccer. When we spotted the police van, we had to run as if our life depended on it. The police would beat us up if they caught us. I have always walked to school. High school was about four miles away. During high school, we frequently went house dancing. Discotheques were very popular. We would play karem and table tennis and listen to music. We would play draughts, dominoes, darts, and rings. We would make whistles from reeds and bamboo. We would fly kites and play yo-yo. We used to walk through the Liesbeeck River to the beach in Milnerton. We used to go cycling, and I worked in a grocery store on Friday and Saturday afternoons. We loved running long distances. Throughout my high school years and beyond, I was aware that I had a strong social conscience. I was very upset by the injustices that I witnessed. I participated in political rallies. Running away from the police was exciting and scary.

During my young adult life, I became the chairperson of Erica Primary School Board and of the Kensington Minister's Fraternal. During this time, I presided over the first ecumenical communion service in our local church in 1975. I was the regional chairperson and vice president of the National Executive Committee (NEC) of a national NGO. I also became the point person for European agencies that were funding projects in South Africa. I continued to organize and speak at political rallies.

Desiree and I got married in 1979, the same year as the Iranian revolution and hostage crisis. It was also the international year of the child and China adopted its one-child policy. I remember snow falling in the Sahara desert for the first time. *Star Trek: The Motion Picture* was released. I remember some of the significant events of this year when Michael Jackson released his *Off the Wall* album and Mother Theresa won the Nobel Peace Prize. Many of these events can still be considered "unfinished business" because they are still in the news almost daily. This was the year when Menachem Begin of Israel and Anwar Sadat of Egypt signed a peace treaty at the White House while President Carter was in office. Bishop Abel Muzorewa became the first black prime minister of Rhodesia, and Saddam Hussein became the president of Iraq. Chrysler (Motor) Corporation asked the U.S. government for a bailout to prevent filing for bankruptcy.

I had to work very hard to be a good parent. I had to constantly keep myself in check so that I did not repeat my childhood in rearing my own children, whom I continue to love dearly. I had to shatter the mold that shaped my life. It was customary in my childhood to get a solid and often undeserved spanking. Children should be seen and not heard was the maxim of the time. Initially, I started disciplining my children the way I was disciplined until I realized that I was doing the same things to my children that I hated as a child. I had to work hard at it. Eventually I ended up with a parenting system that worked for me. I was my children's comforter from birth until they were about two. I would love them unconditionally and provide for their needs without them having to deserve anything that I did for them. I was compelled to comfort them by virtue of my parent status. Later on, I was my children's constabulary. I had to make sure that they do things right as well as do the right things. I would make sure that they knew the logical and natural consequences of their commission as well as their omission. I would drill them to understand the way life works until they were about ten. I knew from my studies that children develop peripheral vision from about nine years of age, and this also tied in with theories about the development of moral consciousness in children. When my children reached ten years of age, I became their coach; I would find out what they could do well, and I would start coaching them to do it better. My wife and I had earlier decided that we would introduce our children to music. We gave them the option to play any musical instrument. Today they can play trumpet, flute, drums, clarinet, trombone, piano, guitar, saxophone, and of course the fool. As they exit adolescence, I take on the role of consultant. They know that even if they do not take my advice, I will still love them unconditionally by virtue of my parent status.

My wife was very passive and subservient to the dictates of the political system at the time. I was always challenging the status quo. I never questioned my right to be; I affirmed it. I never obeyed those directive apartheid signs that reserved doors, spaces, and seats for whites. I challenged and almost always survived. I was very militant. I was the first person of color who was allowed to attend a prestigious institution of higher learning. I did not allow anyone to superimpose their thinking onto my face. I did not question my right to be where I was and to do what I was doing. I moved with steadfast decisiveness. I always tried to affirm this right, and this got me into lots of trouble. I believed that I am a person in my own right. I was stubborn. When they said that I should go to the back door of the store to get service or attention, I just left, knowing that my money had purchasing power. However, when I left, the reality confirmed that I did not get what I wanted and this spawned more conflict.

One of the first disagreements that my wife and I had about child rearing was about buying clothes for our firstborn son, John. I always bought baby clothes to fit exactly—not one inch too big. Why? I was sick and fed up with always having clothes that were too big for me. Clothes were always handed down to me. These clothes caused me to be ridiculed by friends and often attracted horrible nicknames. I had no control over the clothes that I wore as a child because I had no buying power. My peers, I guess, never understood this, or maybe they were hiding their own feelings of inferiority behind the act of poking fun at me. I usually ended up beating them up and getting into more trouble, and they grinned at the success at getting me into trouble. I grew up with a deeply ingrained philosophy of "having to make do." I knew too well what to say when I did not have what I was supposed to have. I guess at some point or other, one develops a poverty complex, and it is a challenge to get out of a poverty-conditioned mind-set.

The government policies made it very difficult for me to rear my children. The conflict engulfed me because I was not sure about what I should teach my children—civil obedience or civil disobedience? Should I teach them to obey the police officers or to disobey the rule of law? What would my peers and colleagues say? One subtle perplexity can be seen from the following illustration. I remember watching a rugby match at Newlands with my eldest son, John, and when the announcement was made that the newly elected national leader F. W. de Klerk had arrived in the stadium, I told my son to stand up with me and acknowledge his presence. My friends and comrades at the time called me a sellout because I was acknowledging F. W., when in fact I was acknowledging his office, which is an important distinction to instill in our children: to respect the office even if we cannot respect the man.

What I have lived through during apartheid was crucial to my later development. I was saddled with feelings of insecurity, anxiety, fear, shame, anger, rejection, guilt, powerlessness, and a general mood of not being good enough. This is a lot of baggage for a child's developing shoulders. I think that people do not really know what happened during the apartheid era. There are stories that have not been told. The pain of people whose stories have not made the annals of the Truth and Reconciliation Committee is no less painful or important. People have thus far focused much on the physical damage. However, the effects of the emotional damage over time will be with us for at least another generation. This generational legacy will be with us for many generations to come.

One of the first things that I had to address as an adult was the stereotype I was generating. In my youthful conflicted state of exuberance and anger, I thought of myself as a cool, devoid of hang-ups, nonjudgmental, easygoing, can-get-along-with-everybody person. I had to check my stereotypes in order to find out how open-minded I really was. I somehow knew that I would not get far by demonizing everybody.

We forget that our thoughts are not discontinuous, momentary happenings; our thoughts are processed and part of a process. This process started with our original, orienting responses, and we have been conditioned by these ever since. What we see and hear shapes us, whether we are aware of it or not. Information, especially the source of the information, is crucial; be it the media, TV, newspaper, or the Internet, this information shapes us. We do not always verify the authenticity of the sources. We accept that if it is in the *New York Times*, then it must be true.

The agendas of news sources, and there are many, will battle to dominate your mind. Most people do not even know that these agendas exist. These sources are often aligned with ideologies and sleek propaganda mechanisms. You have to consciously focus and reflect on what has gone into your mind. Whatever garbage has gone in will come out; whatever good has gone in will come out. Your mind is powerful, and you are responsible for what you feed it. You watch a particular advertisement on television and believe their pitch. You then go out and buy it. If you feed your mind that fatty food tastes good, you will believe it and eat it and will soon end up with chronic ill health, being obese, and feeling miserable. Likewise, if you believe that people are inferior, you will treat them accordingly. Your perception ultimately drives your interaction with life. Feeding bad thoughts produces more bad thoughts.

Could I have been wrong all this time? My mom told me, and she cannot be wrong. We have always done it this way because it is our tradition, our culture, our faith. Your current lifestyle has been influenced since your socialization as a child. Unless you stop to reassess your innermost thoughts, you might be saddled with some unintended consequences. This process can be painful. Pain, however, can produce a new resolve, a new purpose.

In spite of the society in which you live, you are solely responsible for the stereotypes that you harbor. You have to take stock of these stereotypes because your perception will determine your interaction with others, especially with other genders, races, and ethnicities different than your own. These stereotypes are spawned in one's family system and carried into the workplace, so society continues to be shaped by the experiential world of your childhood. Hence it is important to engage in reflective practice continuously.

I would find the answer to some of the conflict of my experiential world of childhood in seeing my work at a residential care facility as a calling. When I saw the conflict in the lives of the children, my conflict began to dissipate. Though I thought that my trauma was the worst of its kind, I saw children who were still smiling in spite of worse crises in their lives. I used to moan that I had no shoes; I stopped because I saw children with no feet. The children, young people, and their families honed my listening skills. I would spend hours just listening to the stories they had to tell. We are so prone in the helping professions to hear the sound of our own voice. The best skill you can practice is to listen actively, with every fiber of your being focused on the ones you serve. You have to connect with your eyes, your ears, and your body. You have to be able to distinguish between their authentic story and a "story." I remember a colleague who was very religious, working with boys in a secure care facility. The boys petitioned a meeting with this director. Permission was granted and they went to his office to share a story. They said that they wanted to be spiritual like he is. They asked him to pray for them. He prayed earnestly for them and their resolve to turn over a new leaf. Well, by the time he said "amen," they had taken the keys, unlocked the gates, and escaped.

The agency that I directed was also a victim of the Group Areas Act. It was founded in District Six in 1868 and was relocated to the Cape Flats. I admitted to the agency, children who had been severely, abused, neglected and traumatized. These children were apartheid's poverty victims. They came mainly from fatherless homes and fractured, high-risk communities—communities that had few if any protective factors that ensured the peace and safety necessary to grow up uninterrupted. Poverty was the greatest causal factor for the disruption of their lives. The cohorts of poverty are alcohol abuse and family violence. These children would be referred to the agency because the mom's boyfriend, for example, decided to throw gasoline on the shack and set it ablaze. The seemingly trivial issues were often the root cause of the uprooting of many children in these poverty zones.

I remember five-year-old twins Kholi and Kholiswa, a boy and a girl, whose grandmother slammed the door, breaking the boy's leg simply because he asked for bread because he was hungry. She had no food to give. Her son, the twins' father, had committed a murder and was on the run from the police. A passerby found them sleeping in a forty-five-gallon drum. Another child came to us because her mother had poured gasoline on her dad because he continuously abused the mother. The mother made that child watch her father die. Some were sexually abused by a parent or family member. Some were AIDS orphans. It was indeed difficult to work with this population because one minute they would be alive and well and the next day they would die.

None of the children had committed a criminal offence. The only offence was against them. No one loved them enough to help them heal their hurts. People often lack patience in working with children and young people who are hurting. People want to fix them and to make them right, instantly. I am pleading for a latitude of tolerance like when you put a rubber band over your index finger and your thumb of your left hand. You then pull at the rubber band with your index finger of your right hand. The idea is that even if the tension increases because of the pull, the rubber should not break. Through a growth producing relationship, open communication and sustainable engagement the tension can be reduced. Latitude of tolerance implies active engagement through an understanding and patient mindset.

It was imperative that I understood the difference between maladaptive and deficient behavior. Maladaptive behavior is when a child has been taught a social behavior but does not have the volition to follow through with the socially accepted behavior. Deficient behavior is when a child has not been taught a behavior. This was particularly important because many of the children came from rural areas where there were no inside bathrooms. They would run outside and urinate behind a tree. They would get punished for this by the staff. I deemed this to be unfair because they first had to be taught to use the water closets of the agency before they could be punished for doing otherwise.

Many children in institutional care become dropouts or outcasts in a rigid system that cannot deal with difference and diversity. These young people who drop out find their belonging needs met by members of gangs, and they get involved in crime. I am not condoning the crimes that they commit but want to remind you that they often cry bullets because the bullets express their anger, their pain, and their tears. If we fail to attach, we fail to develop meaning. We need to connect with children in spite of our perceived differences. We need to learn to celebrate our diversity. We should not insist that others always have to conform to our way of life and lifestyle. Many interpersonal conflicts and arguments are spawned by this "to be" lifestyle. Does this lifestyle attest to the fact that we may be control freaks or, at best, that we are still playing power games? Our biggest problem in working with emotionally disturbed children from high-risk environments is the "to be" problem. We want them "to be" sweet, well-behaved, obedient, compliant, charming, clever, pretty, well-dressed. We will do so much for them if they were "to be" . . . and this translates equally powerfully into our interactions and communications with families, educators, social workers, and stakeholders. We would learn a lot more about life if we can observe, i.e., take in and not subject, for that means controlling and directing the lives of others according to our specifications. In the process, we lose a lot of the awareness, spontaneity, and intimacy—in fact we lose out on life and meaningful living. In the process of adult manipulation, children do not just get wary of the adults; they become amused at the fact that the longer we argue with them, the younger the adults become. Adults regress automatically and often lose their cool. When a child is out of control or in a crisis, the only thing worse for the child is an adult who spirals out of control. In many countries, we are failing because we have stopped listening to the voice of the voiceless masses . . . our children. They cannot vote? Is that why they are not first on our agenda? Working with children and youth, developmentally, in a therapeutic milieu or nurturing environment is the only fair, fruitful, functional, firm, formative, and fun way of interacting with and responding to them. We have to stop using our medical disease or pathology model and utilize an asset-based approach. We can do more for children based on their strengths than on their deficits. Sometimes we focus on what a child or young person has not done while ignoring all the things that they have done successfully. They could wash, dress, brush their teeth, comb their hair, and then you can only notice the one button on their shirt that is undone. When we focus on their assets or strength or what they can do, we will notice that they can do so much more with a little bit of momentary hurdle help.

I completed the first master's degree study in residential care in post-apartheid South Africa and became the first person with a doctoral degree in child and youth studies in South Africa. In my master's thesis, I focused on family reunification because we had a different kind of lost generation in South Africa. In the dark ages of apartheid, the regime removed children from their families. In this study, I found that more than 54 percent of the children and young people were in residential care, away from their families for more than two years. The idea was that the families were incompetent to care for their children and that children were better off in a residential care facility. They thus punished the family by placing the children in facilities away from their families and homes. The problem was that over time, the children and their families lost contact with each other. In the same manner, families could not afford the cost of transport to visit their children. Families thus lost interest in their children over time. Some children stayed in the agency until age eighteen, when they were legally able to terminate the welfare services. We designed a family reunification program to reunite families with their "lost" children. Sometimes we would find the family and witness the family denying the relationship with the child. Children were rejected, insulted, and blamed for the disruption of family life. On our way back from the family home in the rural areas, the children would always fall asleep as a way to mask their pain.

Once a year, we would have a huge family picnic. The Golden Arrow Bus Company donated buses that would take all the families and their children to the beach. Food for the day was donated. We played games and had fun. We also took all the children to the carnival on the Goodwood Agricultural Show Grounds. This is the current site of Grandwest Casino. We never had a bad incident during these outings. In my reading for my doctoral degree, I inquired about the therapeutic value of agencies in a post-apartheid era. Much of the Organizabonding Model that I later developed is based on my research findings. I will discuss this model in chapter 7.

I am still in direct contact with many of those children and young people who are now adults and many of whom have children of their own. I remember a girl who had constant nightmares because she witnessed a gang attempting to rape her mother. She called their attention to herself in the hope of saving her mother. She had to run for her life and had to be moved out of the neighborhood because her life was in danger. The mother later befriended the gang and had a child with one of them. The girl had to be transferred to yet another facility for her own safety.

I also remember a boy who had continuous trouble with a specific teacher at school. He was the product of rape. His white mother was raped by a black farmworker. Society expected the white family to hide their shame. Subsequently they banished their daughter from the farm. The daughter in turn banished her son from her life. I later found out that this teacher was severely harsh with this boy because she too was the product of rape.

Then there was a six-year-old girl who was sexually abused by her dad. Upon investigation, I found that the girl's stepmother knew about it but did not report it, her excuse being that it was not happening to her own daughter. She rationalized that he was the father and he had the right to do to his daughter as he pleased.

On one occasion, the clinical social worker and I were cofacilitating group work with fifteen girls who were victims of sexual abuse. I remember that we were talking about sex, secrets, and relationships. I was asking them to define a healthy relationship. The girl sitting next to me insisted that I go first, and because there is no rank order in group work, I started rambling on and on about relationships. I described how my wife and I would walk barefoot on the beach. I described how we would sit down back to back while sipping cocktails and reading an engrossing book. Every so often, we would kiss and exchange a loving glance. The girl next to me could contain herself no longer, and she blurted out, "What, no sex?" In an unguarded moment, I responded by saying how long does it last anyway. She was quick to point out that now they all knew that I was not using Viagra.

Our work with the Child and Family Reunification Initiative often took us to farming communities in the rural areas. Here I discovered a horrendous practice. Families, mainly colored families, were essentially trapped slaves on these farms. They would pick the fruit and work for the white farmer. At the end of the day, they would form a line, and the farmer would fill the enamel jugs that they were holding with cheap wine like Lieberstein or Oom Tas or Soetes (sweets). This was known as the *tot* system (*dopstelsel*). The farmer would give the families rations of tea, sugar, rice, maize flour, and coffee. The farmer gave them just too little so that they would have to borrow money to buy more food. In any event, they could only buy their food at the farm store on the farm. In this way, they ran up debt with the farmer. The meager wages that they got were not enough to make a living, let alone pay back the loan. The children of these families became the property of the farmers. These children were often recipients of a double whammy. They would be abused by their own families as well as by the farmer and his family. I remember being ordered off such farms at gunpoint and a few well-chosen superlatives by the farmer. Incest was rife, and pretty girls were prime targets. The ills that children suffered are too painful to record. One boy was tied to a chain in a cow pad and forced to eat the cow dung by the farmer for misbehavior. His parents had no say over the little boy's plight.

And then there was Norman Afzal Simons with whom I worked at the children's home. Norman's services were terminated. He was later found guilty of the serial killing of twenty-one boys under the age of eleven. He sodomized the boys before strangling them. I remember him asking me where the people were when his dad was sodomizing him for eight years. Pain grooves your life. You get trapped in the pain, and the pain leaves its mark on your body, mind, and soul. Often pain is a precursor to an identity in crisis.

In a sense, we all travel through this life once only. Turbulence in one's life can be an awkward challenge. I am a regular traveler. I know the familiar refrain before every departure from the terminal building, "In the event of a gradual loss of cabin pressure, oxygen masks will drop from the panel above your head. Please, place the mask over your own nose and mouth, then assist others . . ." It is indeed when people in pain do not have the skill sets to secure their own survival that they pose a risk to others. Clarity and conviction about one's identity is an essential component of survival. I have witnessed so many people who damaged themselves and others because they did not have access to a life-sustaining oxygen mask. Sometimes, they just need to regulate their breathing or know that someone cares.

Chapter Three

Identity Crisis

Through others, we become ourselves.

—Lev "Leon" Semyonovich Vygotsky (1896-1934)

I often wondered who I was, where I came from, and where I was going to. One's sense of identity is crucial in negotiating this world. Your identity is the wellspring of what you do and what you want to be. See, what you do is the "deeds narrative" or expression of your identity or who you are. Who you are is then expressed in what you do and what you "be" in the context of your reality. If your dad becomes violently sick, vomits, and bleeds, you will, in spite of how you feel about blood and vomit, do what is needed because love has created a parent-child relational identity between your dad and you. So you see yourself in what you are prepared to do and be. In spite of an unacceptable reality of vomit and blood, your identity of being his child will fortify you to do what is needed. Doing what is needed entrenches the sense of community. This doing and being galvanizes the "you" in communion with others because through others, we find ourselves. We do both the things we want to do and do not want to do mostly in tandem with our sense of identity. Identity is akin to finding your voice in your reality. Who I am or who I perceive myself to be is my voice. Sometimes our voice can be disabled as we are disconnected from others. Identity should find expression in the reality because that is how community is created. We have authentic community when we all have a voice.

I was forced by often hostile forces to reflect, rethink and realize who I was in this global village. I came from a culture where I was taught by my beloved mom that I am because other people are. She often said that we do not have much but we are always ready to share and others will be ready to share with us from what they have. In that way we can all survive. Ubuntu, community, collective mindset, engagement and a strong sense of belonging anchored my life. My identity was not about me and who I was but whose I was in relationship with others. This relational philosophy was often deemed to be a primitive African mindset. I knew that something was different when during my first visit abroad I met people who were steeped in a culture of mine, me and I. The people that I met were focused on personal space and power and control. My parents taught me about ours, we and us. They taught me about soft power that is the only power that does not seek to destroy others but rather to include others through dialogue, invitation and inclusion. Soft power is the power of the soft answer that defuses the conflict and anger. Soft power is when you can destroy your opponent but don't because you realize that your opponent is in fact a real person that is sharing the world and its resources with you. If we continue to seek the destruction of others, we will eventually destroy the only world we have.

Immigration and the relocation to a new land start you on a journey to find your place in a community, your new reality, and your reworked identity. Immigration then is the search for voice in a new reality. My family and I immigrated and relocated to Fort Lauderdale, Florida, in the United States of America from Belhar in the Western Cape Province on November 18, 2001. My second eldest son accompanied me on this journey. My wife and two more children arrived on December 16, 2001. My eldest son worked as an air traffic controller at Johannesburg International Airport and stayed on in Kempton Park, South Africa, because he was not allowed on our H1-B visa because of his age. We left behind my brother and three sisters and their families, my wife's mom, dad, her brothers and sister and their families. We left behind a known world for an unknown world.

I had hoped to leave behind the trauma of my childhood. I hoped to leave behind the trauma of the attempted car hijacking of my only daughter at age eleven on July 11, 2001. She begged me to give permission for her to have her first sleepover with a friend in her grade at school. I was reluctant, and then she threw the usual unfairness principle at me. She asked why I was letting her brothers do sleepovers but not her. I tried to convince her that fairness is not sameness. I remember saying to her that if she needed panties, I would buy them, and if her brothers needed boxer shorts, I would buy them because fairness implies that I respond to their specific needs. However, if she wanted sameness, it would mean that I would have to buy panties or boxer shorts for all of them. Working with abused children in South Africa has heightened my awareness of the risk factors. I knew that children were often abused by people close to them, people whom they knew like family and friends. The fact of the matter is that I lost the argument; in fact, I have never seen an adult win an argument with an adolescent. She went to her friend after school. Her friend's mom took the two of them shopping and to see an afternoon movie at Tygervalley Shopping Mall in Tygerberg. After the movie was over, they took the back streets home instead of travelling on the National Highway (N1). They arrived home after the movie; the automatic garage door opened, they entered and got out of the car. They started to take out the groceries, and suddenly, they had company in the garage. Four black youths with guns were in the garage with them. After much panic, pleading, and pure fear, the mob left with their jewelry, car, and the groceries that they had just bought.

I had hoped to leave this all behind. However, once a South African, you will always be a South African, because the yearning to be back in South Africa is ever present. You miss your family. You miss your friends. You miss your prayer partners and members of the household of faith. You miss your colleagues. You miss your lifestyle. You miss your volleyball and fishing. You miss your soul food. You miss the sounds, the smells, the sights, and the spaces of your homeland.

The struggle to leave behind a country, family, and friends paled in comparison to an emerging new struggle—a struggle for identity in a foreign land. My identity crisis reemerged. In South Africa, I knew who I was supposed to be. In America, my struggle was a struggle to fit in and conform. It was painfully difficult to know and practice a sense of belonging. Years of socialization in South Africa did not prepare me for life in the United States of America. America is a country where economic power is king, queen, and checkmate; either you have money and power or you don't. There is no grace in between. Relocating to America was something my children often lamented as a bad idea. In South Africa, we were considered upper-middle class. We lived in a nice neighborhood, had a nice, cozy, six-bedroom house, two cocker spaniels, and thirty-five rabbits; our children went to private schools, and I was driving the latest model car. Let me hasten to say that generally people were friendly and supportive in America. My executive dean donated a piano, others furniture, and utensils, and the church gave us a car, a Ford Taurus.

However, the reality of the relocation was the challenge to belong and to find a sense of community. Belonging was difficult with little or no economic power. During the first years, we traveled a lonely road to church, to work, to school, and to home. If you wanted to go anywhere, it cost money. My children had to fit in and find their way in school, and they would often come back from school in tears because their classmates were making fun of Africa. They were asking my children questions about whether lions and wild animals still walked in our city streets. They were asking whether a jumbo jet could land in South Africa. They were asking whether we lived in huts and whether we had running water and electricity. They were asking my children why they say they come from Africa when they are not black. I had to ensure that my children were dressing appropriately so as not to stand out as foreigners. In South Africa, we would never wear socks and flip-flops. In South Florida though, some kids do. When I asked them why, they said it was to keep the mosquitoes away from their ankles. We had to get rid of the suits for my boys because their friends would just wear casual clothes to church. They no longer wear a tie and my daughter no longer wears ribbons in her hair.

I started to relive the trauma of my past. The interesting thing was that no one else questioned or doubted my identity, but I did. I had to get to the place where I could reaffirm who I was. We have been in America for eight years now, and generally, it is getting better except for the current economic crisis. My children are embedded in society; they speak like Americans, have adopted an "American" culture, and are doing well academically, socially, and economically. They have many friends and like to go bowling or to the movies. Eating out is their favorite pastime.

Relocating to another country is never easy because you have to rework and renegotiate your identity, your life, your lifestyle, and your worldview. You have to reestablish friendships and build community. This can be difficult if the culture that you come from is markedly different from the one you intend to embrace. South Africa has a very high-context culture where group identity is the norm. Everybody knows or pretends to know something about everybody else's business, and the group that you belong to is the important focal point. America by contrast is very low-context. Everyone minds their own business. Here you have to fend for yourself. You do not speak to strangers, and even your neighbors are strangers. We are fortunate to be living in a nice neighborhood with the best neighbors.

Some of the challenges inherent in relocation can be awkward to negotiate. Children serve an important mentoring function. I have often marveled at how the children become the interpreters of language to their non-English-speaking immigrant parents. Our children became the role models for learning a new lifestyle in a new land. Some of our values had to be redefined and reinterpreted. They continue to teach us about Thanksgiving, Independence Day, President's Day, Martin Luther King Day, and other festivities and events of historical importance. I am still baffled by the millions of dollars Americans blow up in fireworks associated with July 4 Independence Day celebrations.

We no longer celebrate second New Year's Day, Easter Monday, and other significant South African days. We can no longer just walk over to friends and neighbors to visit, to chat, or just to have tea. It is either call first or we will call you to come and visit. When you are invited to lunch or dinner, it is not a treat you have to pay for yourself. Reciprocation is important to energize friendships. Sometimes you cannot start with exploratory dialogues because people can be impatient to listen to stories; perhaps they do not want to skip a beat in their quest to be successful in life. I have found some Americans to be very friendly and supportive, but very ignorant about life beyond the borders of their country. They will help as long as they can see the need to get involved.

God bless America, with its ever-growing immigrant population. We need to reach across diverse barriers to strengthen our growing friendships. We must do for all America's people what they need and stop focusing and satisfying only our greed. Our greed precludes us from identifying need. In the process, we sometimes forget that we do have needs.

We are here to cocreate a country worth living in for all. There are so many people that are lonely around you, wherever you are. We sometimes become so self-absorbed that we do not even notice the pain in the lives of others. They may be grieving the loss of a husband, wife, child, or parent. It is painful to be an immigrant and not to have a moral support system at least. You can only turn to your neighbors and not-yet friends for support in your adopted country. Yet there are so many citizens who do not even know that they are important in the lives of others, most notably foreigners or newcomers to their town or neighborhood. Why don't we do something to build real community? Why don't we reach out to others? I think that this downturn in the economy is a perfect opportunity to reestablish our relationships. This is an opportunity, and opportunity means nothing if we do not act. Maybe we should just start to greet our neighbors in the morning or when we pass each other in the mall, on the road, or at the convenience store. We should just make a commitment to be nice and to treat others with respect.

We, my family and I, have thus far visited eighteen states in our quest to get to know as much as we can about our new country and home. We are engaging in community activities and are involved in a variety of service projects.

The last time that I visited South Africa was during a trip that included visits to Botswana, Zambia, and Zimbabwe in September-October 2008. I was in South Africa at the time of the presidential musical chairs when the beat of a different drum dictated the demise of the president of the Republic of South Africa Thabo Mvuyelwa Mbeki and the rise of Kgalema Petrus Motlanthe, the deputy president of the African National Congress (ANC), as the newly appointed president of South Africa. Talking about presidential musical chairs is a good segue to talk about colored musical chairs.

As I approach this next chapter, I want to salute the role that the late senator Edward Kennedy played in the liberation of oppressed South Africans. After his visit to South Africa in January 1985, he introduced the Anti-Apartheid Act in 1986. This act had the support of Democrats and Republicans, and this support was strong enough to override the presidential veto of President Reagan. This was indeed an historic override. The economic sanctions that followed brought the apartheid regime to a fall. This vision of Senator Ted Kennedy ensured that I and millions of oppressed South Africans could regain our dignity and our identity. This manuscript went to the publisher in the same week of the death of this great elder statesman, Senator Edward Moore Kennedy. Millions of freed peoples around the world attest to his legacy of being the strong politician for others less fortunate. Senator Kennedy saw the political, social, and economic plight of black, colored, and Indian people in South Africa. His political skill sets knew no boundaries. He served the needs of people around the world through his presence in the United States Senate in Washington DC. Millions around the world can claim him as their senator.

Chapter Four

The Political Plight of the Colored People in South Africa

No oppressive order could permit the oppressed to begin to question: Why?

—Paulo Freire (1921-1997)

The Basil D'Oliveira saga is such a snapshot of the reality of colored people in South Africa. Basil Lewis D'Oliveira (Dolly) was born a child of mixed race, and raised as a second class citizen in Cape Town. He was classified as "colored" under the apartheid regime. He was one of the 10 best South African cricketers of the century. Dolly could never play cricket for South Africa because of the brown color of his skin. However, he excelled and was good enough to play for England. When England included him in their touring team to South Africa in the 1968-1969 series, he was denied entry into South Africa by then Prime Minister B.J. Vorster. This refusal to allow Dolly to play for England in South Africa also meant the end of South Africa's sporting ties until 1994. The Dolly syndrome still plays out in sports.

Colored people constitute about 10 percent of the population of South Africa, and they are in the majority in the Western Cape Province and in the Northern Cape Province.

Coloreds were almost at the bottom of the social ladder created by the typology mentioned earlier. Coloreds often had long sleek hair and sharp facial features. Coloreds usually mockingly drew a distinction between sleek hair called *stillaylay* and short curly hair called "stressed" or "pressed" because this kind of hair would be treated with a hot iron and brown paper. Coloreds, generally speaking, were not really business-minded or actively involved in commerce, economics, or politics.

In spite of the lineage of my parents, the one-drop-of-black-blood rule applied in South Africa. A child born from a white father and colored mother was deemed colored. A child born from a white mother and a colored father was deemed colored. In this sense then, my family was considered to be not white, but colored. In fact, on both my mom and dad's side, our family is comprised of about 47 percent colored, 44 percent white, 3 percent Indian, and 6 percent black.

With splits like these, the conflicting images run deep in my political mind-set because of what we as a family had to endure on the receiving end of the apartheid ideology. We were made poor. Our land was expropriated. One of my dad's friends vowed that the regime can take his land over his dead body. Well, on the day that they served him his papers, he had a heart attack and died. They just continued to throw his family out of their house.

We were always scared of the police because they were brutal. They were not approachable and definitely not friendly. They were particularly brutal during political unrest and riots, often coming after defenseless people in their yellow caspirs and buffels (army vehicles). At the time of the Trojan Horse Massacre on October 15, 1985, in Belgravia Road, Athlone, some colored young people were killed and many others were injured. The life of a colored person had no value or sanctity, and death was simply the removal of yet another worthless human being. The Trojan Horse Massacre served the same purpose as it did for the Greeks of old. The riot police were hiding in a box on the back of an ordinary truck and opened fire on unsuspecting protestors.

I was always perplexed and asked so many of my white colleagues to explain how F. W. De Klerk, the last president of the apartheid regime, could lead the prayers in his church on Orange Drive Cape Town on a Sunday and order his bulldozers to roll over the shanties (makeshift houses constructed of plastic, cardboard, and other waste building materials) of the blacks, often rolling them into the rubble should they protest. I could not understand church and its message of redemption. I could not understand the "God is love" message. People like Prime Minister Dr. Daniel Francois Malan, a respected pastor in the Dutch Reformed Church before he became prime minister of South Africa in 1948, increased the frequency and intensity of my conflict. I was deeply disturbed at the inhumane policies that he was ushering in against people of color. The older I got, the more troubled I became about their draconian actions. I remember that we had to line up and stand with national party flags in our hands as the train carrying his corpse passed by.

People like Johannes Gerhardus Strijdom, another educated churchman, contributed to my confusion. Hendrik French Verwoerd had a doctorate in sociology and was the cruelest of them all. I was delighted when he was assassinated with a knife by Dimitri Tsafendas on September 6, 1966. Another confusing figure was Balthazar Johannes Vorster, whose brother Koot was the moderator of the Dutch Reformed Church. Is church not about love for God and love for your neighbor? Is church not about redeeming and rebuilding lives? How can you preach about a God of love and then destroy the very creation of the Creator just because of their skin color or complexion?

When the Mandela government came to power, we thought that we were finally going to take our revenge, but President Mandela said that if we do to them, meaning the whites, what they did to us, what better would we be than them? I was equally perturbed when President Mandela went to the house of Betsy Verwoerd for tea in Orania when she refused to come to his residence for tea. His rationale was that we needed everyone's input if we were to rebuild the nation.

Well, the romantic honeymoon is now over. All South Africans are now facing the political reality. Violence and abuse are increasing, unabated. At times it seems as if there is no political will to stem the tide of crime and violence.

I know that the politicians in the governing party, the African National Congress, want us to believe that their aim for the country is a nonracial society. They tout the nonracial policy at every rally, gathering, and on every billboard. They sing the praises of their almost royally perceived nonracial society that is seemingly in place already just because the ANC is in power. The nonracial mantra can be very useful in the hands of a skilled conductor. The skilled conductor can even find the lyrics, or policies, to match the nice-sounding tune. The nonracial concept, to the best of my knowledge and belief, is being used too soon and too much in South Africa. The current reality in South Africa supports this notion. South Africa still has glaring racial problems and tensions. These tensions are alive in the lives of colored people. There are still far too many covert and overt operations driven by race. Contrariwise, I am still unsure why so many black politicians traded in their black wives for a white wife. Is it love, is it color, is it status, is it still economically more viable, more expedient?

The nonracial theme euphemizes the continuing negative statistics, and that is great for the politicians in power. To cover the country under the nonracial blanket means that politicians no longer have to address the issues at the source. Let's face it, apartheid left a legacy. One of the legacies of the Group Areas Act is that people are still grouped together in crime-ridden areas. Crime in the black and colored apartheid-created communities is still rife. Covering crime statistics with the nonracial blanket is not good for the country. Why can we not face the facts, the reality? It is not a shame to confront the legacy of a past that created many demons.

This nonracial manifesto is not doing much for education. The matriculation results continue to be disappointing. Young people en masse in the colored communities are not very motivated. One thing for sure is that the difficulty to get into a tertiary institution to continue one's education or to find a job does not bode well for the improvement of the matriculation results.

Did I say nonracial or a one-race society? I am not an anthropologist, sociologist, or some expert to know that many have tried and failed to sell the idea of a nonracial society. Honestly, in the final analysis, it is really looking like a one-race society with policies like Black Economic Empowerment or BEE because it means exactly what it says—black. Colored people are neither benefitting from nor included in the BEE policy framework. Where are the significant housing, electrification, and/or water development for colored people? Now let's be fair that of course colored people benefited, but only to the extent that they were geographically in the same vicinity as a project where blacks constituted the majority. It is indeed easy to advertise a nonracial society as long one race is benefitting unfairly. If a nonracial society is the standard, then why do we have to have Black Economic Empowerment? Should it then not be economic empowerment for all? Should all South Africans not be included in the nonracial society? Yes, but historically speaking, blacks were disadvantaged and government is attempting to level the playing fields for blacks. Blacks have to be politically empowered. You are guilty of double standards because under the same rules by which blacks were disadvantaged, colored people also were disadvantaged.

I will address and try to elucidate the issue of colored people in a South African context. Since 1994 it has really looked like the needs and aspirations of colored people were not a priority to the ANC, the legitimate government of South Africa. Colored people had been in South Africa long before the ANC came to power. There are as many deniers of the history of the colored people as there are people who are interpreting the history of the colored people to prove their own ideology and agenda. How can you conclusively prove anything if the source documents have been contaminated by a previous political regime? They were there since time immemorial. The Khoi-Khoi and the San people were found to be there when Van Riebeeck arrived in Cape Town on April 6, 1652, on his three ships, the *Reijger*, *Drommedaris*, and *Goede Hoop*. Should they and their descendants not be considered and be given the same rights as other indigenous peoples, first nations, or aboriginals? Their existence and identity was a problem since their primary encounter with foreigners to this day. Originally they were referred to as "the bastards" until they were finally being called "Cape coloreds" in 1834. Whites have always seen coloreds as bastards and as illegitimate. The white regime under Strijdom removed coloreds from the Electoral Roll in February 1956. The apartheid regime commissioned different task groups to help define the coloreds, and to this day, no one has succeeded. Long after the National Party was declared rigor mortis, the effects of its ill-conceived racist political schemes are still having an impact on the life of colored people. Even I grew tired of being told who I was.

May I remind you that the apartheid regime had the Immorality Act, Act No. 5 of 1927, in place from 1950-1985? This law made sexual intercourse across the color line a criminal offence. The Immorality Act licensed the police to hunt down couples suspected of being in relationships across the color line. They invaded homes, smashed down doors, and any mixed couple found having sex in bed was arrested. They used the underwear as forensic evidence in court. Couples were almost always given a prison sentence. The colored person was always given the harsher sentence. This was no joke, but it was comical, to say the least, to read the newspaper reports covering the courts and the Immorality Act. Ironically, the first person caught under this act was a white Dutch Reformed Church minister who had sexual intercourse with his colored maid.

The authorities had to force people to believe that miscegenation was not a possible solution to explain the issue of the colored people. They concealed the history of the colored people. Concealing the history of a people is a grievous crime against humanity. The history of colored people have been so distorted and reinvented that it is difficult to get even close to the truth. This has made colored people apathetic to their ancestry, identity, and sadly enough, their political future. Ask any colored person about their identity and notice their discomfort, awkwardness, and clumsiness. The will quickly change the topic. They forget that that which you try hardest to conceal, you most obviously reveal.

Young people, my own family, my cousins, nieces and nephews all show the same reluctance to confront their history because they do not want to be descendants of the Bushmen, Hottentots, and Beachcombers. They do not want to be associated with the "coon carnival" culture. This culture was brought to Cape Town by the Malays. It is similar to the coon carnival in Brazil where people would paint their faces and wear colorful clothes. Usually it is associated with merriment and drunkenness. They do not want to be seen as the bastards or illegitimate offspring of the whites. They know that coloreds were the "poor whites" of the apartheid era. They question where they are coming from. They lament that they have no culture and that they have no real history. To be a colored person is to ask in the present continuous tense, "Who am I? Who am I?" I know of many colored people who are now feeling that they were better off under the apartheid rule.

The pain inflicted by the current political system is becoming unbearable, and it pales in comparison with the pain inflicted by the apartheid era. Everybody knew that apartheid had to end and that the struggle would bring about liberation. How can a nation really be free when some of its legitimate citizens are still suffering because of the color of their skin? Colored people do remember the shackles of apartheid. With all the laws, regulations, and restrictions imposed on colored people, it felt as if the regime was vaccinating colored people so as not to expose the whites to risk. Were the whites morally weak and incompetent to hold their own? Is that why the regime was so harsh in enforcing the law and in exacting and extracting the last ounce of decency that colored people had left in them? All my life I felt as if the whites were being quarantined because they carried the antisocial disease. I felt that the laws were promulgated to keep the whites away from people of color. In the final analysis, both parties missed out on the benefits of engaging with each other.

The search for the history of the colored people has been thwarted by the whites in the National Party who were in power 1948-1994 with a political agenda, the apartheid ideology. Even the most diligent search and analysis is hampered by pseudo-documents and evidence that has been "planted" and "doctored" by this regime in order to legitimize their apartheid quest. They were never found guilty of committing genocide. They were far too smart because the refiner of the draconian apartheid lifestyle, with benefits for whites only, at least had a doctoral degree in sociology. They simply obliterated the history of a people and, in so doing, altered the historical trajectory of the colored people of South Africa. Once they made colored people doubt their history, they could use them like chattel and utensils, at will, to reach their political ends. The only sure thing that they left coloreds with was contempt for themselves. They killed an indigenous nation, and should they not have been found guilty of natiocide? The world remembers atrocities like the Holocaust but does not even engage in dialogues about what has happened and is continuing to happen to the colored people in South Africa. We talk about Buchenwald but not District Six, Cape Town. We talk about the oppression of Native Americans, we talk about the Maoris, we talk about the aboriginals, but nobody talks about what happened to the colored people. Is the world part of the conspiracy in devaluing what has happened to the colored people? Is what happened of lesser importance because no conventional weapons were used?

Let me remind you that the impact and effects of emotional abuse are much, much worse than those of physical abuse. You can slap me and the burn on my cheek will soon be over, but humiliating me and insulting me will leave indelible scars. The colored people do not even talk about their pain anymore. Why? Has this legacy of apartheid altered the genes of colored people to the extent that it has created a generation gap? I do believe that colored people are not in South Africa by chance. I do believe that they have a purpose.

We are dealing with human beings on whose memories are etched, often in blood and pain, the images of their (our) past. They have been uprooted as a result of the Group Areas Act. They have been overlooked for job promotion. They have been culturally isolated. They have been abused. These events and issues are grooved and unless the grooves are filled with positive experiences, now, that can help us transcend our past; we are doomed to stay in the groove. How much more pain, embarrassment, and insult do we expect colored people to endure? How much longer will colored people allow themselves to be marginalized and abused as political pawns? My problem goes to the heart of politics in South Africa.

Can one fell political sweep disintegrate a typology that seems to have existed for so long? Is it not going to take time? Will the mental structures that have been etched in our mind through a process of deliberate socialization over time come tumbling down with just politics and a political policy and/or intervention? See, as long as there are the haves and have-nots, as long as there are the power holders and the powerless, as long as there are the too rich and the too poor, as long as there are the power biters and the power bitten, as long as there is unequal distribution of resources, the nonracial society remains a Utopian dream. Current conditions in South Africa would indicate that we are definitely en route to a one-race society but not a nonracial society.

Colored (*bruinmense*, "brown people") people were always selling each other out, especially to the whites. If you wanted advancement in your job, you had better be nice to your manager who was always white. When colored people were promoted to positions of authority and management, they were real show-offs who delighted in lording it over other coloreds. Services by coloreds became worse for the coloreds being served.

Whites were revered in the society, and at one time, a colored police officer could not ticket or arrest a white person. The whites abused the coloreds at their whim. They knew they could get the coloreds to give them the information that they wanted, and at one point, there were talks of giving the coloreds a vote and they even developed a Colored Persons Representative Council (CRC) with their own parliament. They had other machinations like the President's Council to keep everybody at bay. People often ask me, how were the minority whites able to keep 70 percent of the population at bay? My answer is brutal force, fear, and a denial of your person, your identity. The worst and most effective strategy was to sow doubt about who we as colored people were. If you do not have an identity, what are you standing up for? For me, as a child, my identity was not about who I am, but whose I am, who claimed responsibility for me. Where did I belong, legitimately or not, where did I belong? The whites often wanted to foist things like the coon carnival and the hawker culture onto colored people. They wanted us to destroy ourselves through drugs and alcohol. Many colored people detested this because they were becoming educated, cultured, and they were regaining the property that had been expropriated and stolen from them.

You will recall that I resided in South Africa until 2001. I cut my teeth in South Africa. I was socialized in South Africa. I was impacted by the ordered chaos. I was there when the government departments were fragmented just because of the different races in South Africa. At one time, there were fourteen departments of education. Every department had its own vision and mission and modus operandi. The answer that you got was dependent upon to whom you directed your question. This was conflicting and added greatly to the complexity of raising your children. At this point, I was happy that I was doing my civic duty in raising my children as best I could.

The fact still remains: colored people were marginalized and relegated to do the dirty work of the whites. One such case in question is the establishment of the South African Cape Colored Corps, a band of cadet soldiers that were pushed to the front line to fight the ANC insurgency on the borders and in particular the Caprivi Strip. The Caprivi Strip is a piece of land in the Chobe Delta between Namibia, Botswana, and South Africa. They sent these colored soldiers to the front lines and across the border to bludgeon Umkhonto we Sizwe, the military wing of the ANC. My mom's brother's daughter's husband was a ranked officer in the SACC and would often boast about his exploits across Bridge 14 in pursuit of the perceived enemy. I never agreed with him about his exploits. The strange thing is that when apartheid ended, that was the end of his career as well. He lost his job, his house, and he gave up his will to work.

I became who I am, not because of apartheid, but in spite of apartheid. Let me confess that I believed in the concept of a nonracial society and aligned myself with the principles and core values of the African National Congress in pursuit of this noble goal and challenge. I lobbied, promoted, influenced, and preached about this nonracial society. Alas and did my people bleed in pursuit of the goal of a nonracial society. I was witness to the continued marginalization of colored people. I saw them applying for jobs and being very hopeful. It was indeed a blessing to be called back for an interview. However, once they went for the personal interview, you could just see the pain on their faces as they heard that they did not make it because the company wanted a black person. Colored people are once again the laughing stock of the nation that respects no one for who they are. There was a time when the *Bilingual School Dictionary* (old copies of it has been recalled) stated that "you are as drunk as a colored teacher." This dictionary is no longer needed because this concept is firmly etched in the mind-set of people in South Africa. No one is even bothering to ask why this was ever in the dictionary. There were other derogatory words like *meit* (colored girl), *jong* or *klong* (colored boy), and *kaffir predikant,* which is a derogatory term for a black pastor in the dictionary that demeaned people based on the color of their skin. They just do not bother to ask why.

I am not sure that blacks are not taking revenge on colored people for their earlier alignment with whites during the apartheid regime's reign of power. I am also not sure that they know about the snide remarks and bad things that were said about blacks like do not smile at a black person because they will steal your white teeth.

The goal to establish a nonracial society in South Africa is not well served by the current political monopoly of the blacks. Are all minority rights and aspirations to be usurped by blacks, and is being black the only aspect that matters? Do other races and minorities have to give up their quest to be a people? Is being black the only aspect that will survive? Not acknowledging and not attending to the issues involving the colored people is not a wise move politically.

The fact of the matter is that there were indigenous people who resembled the current descendents called Cape colored or *bruinmense* (brown people) in existence in South Africa before the southward expansion of the black people. These people are still present to this day. The whites denied this fact by inserting derogatory connotations to the terms Khoi, San, Bushmen, Hottentots, and the like. This made a people despise its heritage. Now I am sure that historians can do a much better job than I can about explaining the march of civilization in South Africa. I can give you a clear example of how whites distorted historical facts and altered maps and geographic locations to suit their apartheid ideology.

When my mom and dad's generation went to school, they were taught about Jan Van Riebeeck and his conquest of the Cape under the banner of the Dutch East India Company

(Vereenigde Oost-Indische Compagnie or VOC) to establish a port for ships sailing around the Cape to pursue the spice trade with the East. When I went to school, I was taught about Jan Van Riebeeck and his wife, Maria De La Quellerie. However, when my son went to school, he was taught about Mr. and Mrs. Van Riebeeck, and this is where the fun starts. Jan Van Riebeeck's statue had always been a lonely figure on the Foreshore at the northwest end of the City of Cape Town. The foreshore is land reclaimed from the sea in 1936-1945 in order to expand the Ben Schoeman Harbor. Maria DeLa Quellerie's statue was at the other end of the City of Cape Town in the Company's Gardens. Now when my son was in first grade, the government relocated the statue of Maria De La Quellerie to the northwest side of town next to that of Jan Van Riebeeck. We referred to Maria as Maria De La Khoi-Khoi because we assumed that she was in fact Khoi-San. We believe that Jan Van Riebeeck and Maria were never married in real life. Their statues were placed next to each other with the clear implication that they were married. Morality was a big issue to the Afrikaner whites.

In our proximity lies our danger. I have learned this lesson from my work with abused children in South Africa. The abuser, the perpetrator, is often someone close to, often related to the victim, the abused. It is often their proximity to each other that makes the abuse possible. It is because of the relatedness, the proximity of husband and wife, that domestic violence is possible. Colored people aligned themselves close enough to whites in the apartheid era to be abused by them. During the 1980s and the intensification of the political struggle for freedom from oppression, colored people aligned themselves closely with blacks, and the result is that colored people have been abused once again. To enter into a relationship of trust with another is to make oneself vulnerable to disappointment. Even worse is to entrust your personal fate into the collective mind-set of the majority and to hope for the best. The disappointment eventually makes one lose hope and direction, courage and purpose. I am perturbed that so much has changed politically, but why does everything still look the same for colored people in South Africa?

In our familiarity lies the contempt. I do not know of any right-minded colored person who did not share in the delight and joy at the release of Nelson Mandela on February 11, 1990. We had so much hope that he would deliver colored people. We expected so much from him, yet history will bear testimony to the fact that he and the ANC did not do much to alleviate the plight of the colored people. We too claimed Mandela. We embraced Madiba. We identified with him. Did we become too familiar with this icon of freedom only to be denied, disappointed, and rejected, again? Should we have held his feet to the fire a bit more? Should we have tempered our reverence for him with holding him more accountable for our plight? His impassioned plea to build the nation duped us into forgetting about our own needs as a people. The delusion of indulgence in freedom ensured our continued poverty, political insignificance, and marginalization.

First and foremost, I am a South African, not an African. A person from France or Italy would take strong exception if you refer to them as Europeans first. They want you to be sure of their nationality. In the same vein, in the international community, people tell me with a smirk that blacks in Africa cannot govern. My equally indignant response is that Africa is like a woman who had been raped multiple times by many different rapists. The woman would somehow lose her sense of self and her identity. Likewise Africa has been raped by the British, the Spanish, the Dutch, the Portuguese, and God knows who else. Africa has been plundered not only of its raw materials, but also of its human capital, and I am sorry to say that no sooner did we get rid of the colonial bastards than we did exactly what they did to us to others. We have not invented the role but have perfected the role of to "lord it over" others. We have learned this role very well to make others feel powerless. It is indeed a fact that if your dad was not affectionate, it is difficult to show affection to your children. Likewise, it is difficult to share power with others if a power-sharing model never included you. I am a South African. At forty years of age, I voted for the first time on a sunny day on April 27, 1994.

Effectively neutering the political voices of minorities does not contribute to nation building. Neutering such abilities with token gestures like giving political office to one or two minority people can assuage the immediate concerns, but does not take away the overall aspiration of a people. For too long, colored people in South Africa have been obliterated and marginalized. Marginalization has usurped the colored people. Marginalization is part of their identity, their persona because with the passage of time colored people have internalized marginalization. The white regime systematically stripped colored people of their dignity, thus effectively neutralizing the political player status of the coloreds. Coloreds remained politically naïve. Concomitant with their loss of dignity coloreds seemingly lost their self-respect. When you lose your dignity, when you lose your identity, when you lose your self-respect, you stop dreaming about the future. Eventually even dreams of a new worldview become stillborn. In spite of Mr. Mandela's request and mandate in 1992 that the ethnicity of colored people be acknowledged politically, I cannot see any good that Mr. Mandela and the Mandela government did for colored people. President Jacob Zuma who is doing very well would do even better if only he would do something tangible in order to inspire and to energize the hearts and minds of the coloreds to actively engage in the political processes. Unless the president can help the coloreds to shed their fear of black rule, the Western Cape will elude the grasp of the ANC.

We were marginalized by the white nationalist government, and we continued to be marginalized to the same degree, extent, and purpose by the current ANC party. Let me humbly submit that one of the reasons why colored people in the Western Cape have not voted for the ANC in large numbers is that the ANC has seemingly done nothing for colored people, or not yet. I know of colored families in my former hometown who have to hunt moles and other wildlife in order to feed their families and to survive. Colored families still have to sell scrap in order to raise money to make ends meet. Informal settlements for coloreds are a burgeoning enterprise. When the government fails to develop urbanization protocols and policies, the people take the law into their own hands. Wealthy people will exploit poor people by allowing them to settle on open pieces of land while they collect rent from these camps. It is a lot like refugee camps. In fact many of them carry the names of refugee camps like Kosovo and Lawaaikamp.

I can no longer look at people who ignore the cause of their own pain. They are in collective denial. I cannot just observe the dripping pain and the continual hijacking of this group of people. It is indeed my prayer and intent that something needs to be done politically to amend this defective landscape.

When will the marginalization and exploitation of colored people stop? It is my hope that the ANC, COPE (the Congress of the People), the newly formed political party in South Africa established recently in the Free State Province, as well as other political parties will acknowledge the existence of colored people and that their collective needs as a people will be addressed. Blacks emphatically state that coloreds are not blacks. The past as well as the current plight of colored people remain an ineluctable casualty of the South African political system. Ignoring this plight will not make it go away.

Colored people should become comfortable with the term colored. Whether they think of this heritage as coming from Saartjie Baartman, or a mixing of the races, the question is whether second—and third-generation coloreds should still grapple with their identity. In Brazil, for example, colored people are just Brazilians. We know that the reason for this identity crisis is one which was perfected by the white regime during the apartheid era. Much more vigorous debate should be encouraged in order for colored people to become comfortable with the designation, colored. The outcome of the latest election on April 22 is an indication that colored people are mobilizing themselves as a political force to be reckoned with because they do have political capital. It will indeed be very difficult for the ANC to win the Western Cape Province as long as the ANC is not doing enough to win the confidence of the colored people in the Western Cape Province. Please do not get me wrong. I am not pleading for separate nation status for colored people. I am not asking for preferential treatment and laws to protect colored people. I am asking that we acknowledge the role that colored people played in the struggle for political freedom. I am asking that we put a stop to the second-class citizenship of colored people. I am asking that we understand the history, identity, and aspirations of the so-called Kleurlinge-Bruinmense colored people. No matter how much we explain and explain and explain the scientific origins of colored people, no matter whether we attribute the term *colored* to the racist policies of the National Party, the fact is that here is a group of people called colored who are being excluded socially and politically, and that is wrong and immoral. Their marginalization is as historical a fact as the Holocaust and other atrocities perpetrated against groups of people.

Simply continuing the disenfranchisement of colored people will not dissipate the relevance of their political and social issues. Continuing the rationalization that there is no biological and scientific basis for a colored people or race does not mean that there is not a group that is being exploited, ignored, and marginalized. Where is the scientific evidence that distinguished Swedes from Norwegians and Danish? Biologically they are not different. However they each are a distinguished people. You will not make one indefinable lump of Swedish, Norwegians, and Danish. They are separate and equal. I am sure that we do not want to continue with the same vitriolic game plan against colored people, simply emulating our former oppressors. Whether covert or overt, the absence of any positive political action to bring coloreds into the political equation suggests that there is a dangerous and likely intentional omission.

Judging by the opening salvos of the 2009 political campaign, the country had to go on alert for any violent uprising, and that in itself is not an expected element in a fifteen-year-old democracy. In a fifteen-year-old democracy, you should embrace peaceful transition of political power through the democratic election process. Every election year, it is indeed my sincere hope that the campaign of the ANC and other parties will not just be more vacuous and desperate in its rhetoric like past campaigns. The country can ill afford the political pandering of the past. The country needs to do something to bring morality back to politics because young people are watching their role models. Having removed the immorality act does not mean that we now have license to become immoral. It is obvious that polygamy does not sit well with the ethics and standards that South Africa has embraced in the past.

The ANC felt the need to remove and to change the names of airports, cities, and streets that reminded the nation of its former oppressors. Verwoerdburg was changed to Centurion, in order to erase the Verwoerd name. Changing names does not change history, and it does not undo what was done. Likewise, changing to a nonracial political culture does not undo the history of people. During my most recent visit to Pretoria, I noticed that the streets and map of the area that were etched on my mind had been altered. Even the aesthetics of the Union Buildings in Pretoria are different. The ANC is doing what the white regime has done in the past to support their ideology. God forbid that we will have to rename cities and airports and streets just to wipe out the memory of a new wave of oppression under the de facto black rule of the ANC.

I humbly submit that there is a group of people in South Africa who are not engaged in the political processes in South Africa at this time. Until and unless the colored people buy into the political processes, they will not contribute to the improvement of the quality of life for all South Africa's peoples. The establishment, no, the government needs to be applauded because the quest for a nonracial society is the right one. However, the timing from a historical perspective is out of synchronization with the facts on the ground. Yes, we are one society, but only until there is a crisis. Why is it that we know that it was coloreds who did not vote for the ANC and that is why the ANC did not win the Western Cape in elections? Was the world not ready to pounce on Islam after the 9/11 attack? Was the world not ready to blame the Arabs? See how our brotherhood and sisterhood is celebrated when things are going well. However, when the crisis comes, we are quick to point fingers at "them" the ones who are different from us, whoever "they" might be.

When I visited South Africa in 2008, I was appalled by the increase in alcohol and drug abuse among colored young people, and in exploratory dialogues with them, I was alarmed at how cynical they had become and how hopeless they were feeling about the present political situation. They pointed to an increase in suicide among their peers. They pointed out the increase in drug abuse of their respected comrades. They said that they were poorer now than during the apartheid era and this when the country's GDP has increased significantly. They were lamenting, "We are being overlooked for jobs because we are too white to be black, and previously we were too black to be white." They attributed the fragmentation and fracturing of family life to rising unemployment statistics among the colored people. Crime against colored people is on the rise. Just this week, we received news from South Africa about a young family member and father of three whose face had been systematically chopped up with a broken bottle. Research study after research study keeps on confronting us about the increase of illegitimate children and teenage pregnancies among coloreds. What do we expect if your means only allow you to live in a one-bedroom house where—no, you are almost forced to be a witness to the everyday pathos, the ebb and flow of the relationship between mom and dad, spouse and spouse, concubine and parent, or just a one-night stand. Sex then is not a matter of choice and of taking responsibility for the relationship, but the mere continuation of a lifestyle. They see how the children of blacks who had been previously disadvantaged continue to line up for benefits and handouts and privileges based on their blackness, when these children are no longer disadvantaged because their parents are now in government and on the boards of mega-conglomerates. They see how affirmative action once again spells out their nonacceptance in society and the political franchise because of the color of their skin. I saw the apartheid pockmarks on the collective mind-set, the lifestyle and the cultural context of South Africans. The truculent implementation of the apartheid ideology continues to spawn vitriolic acts among the peoples and races in South Africa. The conflicting images continue. When will day dawn and the breakthrough come for coloreds? When will colored people take up their rightful place in South African society? Nobody is going to afford them these rights and privileges. Colored people will have to learn to stand together and do for themselves what is needed most. We have to say enough, no more. We will not allow anyone to overlook us and tell us we do not qualify because we are not black. We will no longer allow people from neighboring states to take jobs for which we are perfectly qualified.

The current avalanche of the financial fallout is cascading over people and their lifestyles. People who had lots of money now have no money. People who had no money now have even less opportunity to get money. Pain is in the faces of millions of unsuspecting families who are unwittingly and unwillingly sucked into this crisis. If something needs to be done as a prerequisite for this nonracial society, then we must tackle poverty. I do not mean redefining it in terms of a World Bank or International Monetary Fund definition. We must put those processes in place that can eradicate poverty. I am sure that we do have economists who can devise comprehensive strategies to at least alleviate the plight of the poor because to be poor is not shameful but is crippling.

Second, we must revisit education and, in particular, school culture, climate, and curriculum. Schools are the biggest social control institutions in the world. More children are being failed *by* the education system in South Africa than children failing *in* the education system. We need the school system to help overcome poverty through education.

Poverty is not a killer; the consequences of poverty are the killer. Poverty forces you in a groove with very few options to escape. Poverty excludes you socially. Poverty means access denied. Poverty forces you to ride the bus and train and to meet people who are equally poor as you. Poverty forces you into the same miserable line at the hospital and at clinics because the people standing in the line are the same as you in that they too have no money. Money forces you to do things that others consider an embarrassment like washing your laundry by hand on a plank in a bathtub. Poverty forces you to mend your clothes and shoes because you cannot afford new ones. My sister and her family knew poverty. She had three beautiful sons and an equally pretty daughter. They did well in school. One day the oldest son just went to buy a car. He just grew tired of being poor. And then the police arrested him because first they said that he wanted to defraud the car dealership. Then they sent him for a psychiatric assessment and found that he was a mental case, although he had showed no signs before of mental disturbance. They roughed him up so badly during this process that he is now a genuine mental case and his brother is equally disillusioned. Can South Africa afford this kind of waste of its prime human resources? In fact, can any nation that is serious about nation building choose to deliberately ignore the needs of some of its citizens? Ignoring some citizens affects all citizens in turn. My biggest concern is the effect that this political neglect of doing the right thing has on the developing minds of its youngest, its future, its voiceless, its most vulnerable, its children.

My dream for people of color in America and in any other place where they are a minority is that they will pick themselves up out of the groove of contentment. I hope that they will stop degrading themselves. I know that it will take courage. I know that after one or two initial setbacks that they will rise and take a stand. It is important that we have a positive disposition. It is important that we stop being our own worst enemy. It is important that we do not install glass ceilings on possibilities and opportunities. People of color should refrain from the entitlement culture. People of color should no longer truckle. People of color should affirm their presence and their right to be. We should know that we do not have to suck up and that we do not have to sell others out in order to advance in life. There is nothing wrong in being a person of color.

I know that many come from family systems that have been dysfunctional for years. I know from experience that it is tough to get beyond the guilt, shame, and embarrassment of our past. I know that if people have told you for years that you *cannot*, it is complicated to start believing that you *can*. You have to do for yourself what you need to do because no one else is going to do it for free. If Mr. Obama can be president, then nothing can stop you from achieving your dreams for yourself.

Society should also play its role in recognizing that it is morally wrong to discriminate against people because of the color of their skin. The bias against people of color has a direct impact on the children of people of color. If a nation continues to marginalize people of color, it is seriously limiting its own resources. We need to remind ourselves that apartheid was a system of keeping colored people in check. This system dictated certain processes like the group areas act and the pass laws. These processes maintained the system. Sometimes we cannot overthrow the system but we can weaken the processes and in so doing bring about meaningful change.

We need to reexamine the processes that grant people access to opportunity. We need to find out if there is a political agenda, bias, or ideology subtly at work. People and groups who want to marginalize others are often very smart at implementing their grand schemes. Once people have been marginalized or rendered politically defunct, it will take generations to correct such heinous schemes. I am very concerned about the impact of apartheid on the next generation of colored people in South Africa because most of the international programs support programs for black empowerment and often the needs and situation of colored people are overlooked in South Africa. As a former director of an NGO in South Africa, I had been turned down so many times for funding because the agency did not have enough black clients in its program. The needs of colored people are equally valid as that of blacks. Again, I do not have the answers, but we should at least open the dialogue about the political plight of the colored people in South Africa. Recently I heard a number of conspiracy theories about coloreds wanting to take over the world since so many current world leaders are so-called colored or biracial.

Chapter Five

Conflicting Images in Our Family System

> *If you don't know [your family's] history, then you don't know anything. You are a leaf that doesn't know it is part of a tree.*
>
> —Michael Crichton (1942-2008)

> *In every conceivable manner, the family is link to our past, bridge to our future.*
>
> —Alex Haley (1921-1992)

Location: → These conflicting images mostly played out on Eighth Street off Fifth Avenue in Kensington. Kensington is a suburb of Maitland Estate in Cape Town. Our house was number 93 and was opposite my grandmother's house, number 86. My grandfather's and his brother's house was on the northwest corner of Eighth Street and Fifth Avenue. The house of my grandfather and his brother was constructed of wood and iron and had three bedrooms, a kitchen, dining room, room for bathing, and an outside toilet, as was typical. My dad's father's house, which he later gave to the church, was a brick structure with five bedrooms, a study, and bathroom and outside toilet. It had a large garden in front. My grandmother's house had a garden in front and a veranda with a grapevine over it; and my grandfather's brother's house had no garden and had a large piece of vacant land to the west of the property.

My dad had three brothers and three sisters. His father was extremely wealthy and had many properties. He gave each child some land. Most of the children lost the land as a result of the Group Areas Act. After the land was expropriated it was zoned for white residential use only. Coloreds had to move. The money that they got for their land was not enough for the down payment on another house in another area. One of my dad's brothers lived next to us in Vasco. He later moved to Bishop Lavis. He was nothing but a drunk when he came back from WWII. He used to abuse his wife regularly. He had two wonderful sons. He had a chicken coop with lots of chickens. One night he awoke in the early hours of the morning with the dog (named Bonzo) barking. Through the window, he saw someone running off with one of his chickens. He ran out outside and gave chase. About halfway down the road, he realized that his bottom was feeling extra cold. It is then that he looked down and discovered that he did not have on anything but his pajama top.

My mom had three brothers and three sisters. This family loved singing. My mom's brothers loved to croon Sinatra songs when they had downed a few whiskey shots. One brother was a clicker in a shoe factory, one was a marine engineer and the other was an auto mechanic. The auto mechanic's son was an auto mechanic as well and immigrated to Australia with his wife and children. After eleven years in Australia, we received news just before Christmas that he had committed suicide. Olive, my mom's youngest sister, was very fair and very pretty. She was a dressmaker. From Olive I learned about the money spinner for colored families called Fah-Fee, which was the thirty-sixth numbered Chinamen's game. Each day a number would be drawn. I remember number 10 was egg, and if you played one penny, you would win twenty-two pennies if your number was drawn for that day (ten pennies is roughly equivalent to one U.S. cent). The game was considered illegal and runners (operators) would be frequently busted.

Albert, my mom's eldest brother, was tall, handsome, light-skinned, and athletically built when he signed up for the army at the age of seventeen in 1939 and served in the Second World War as a bugler. He was very aware of his good looks. He went to war at the same time as his friend Lloyd who I will talk about later on. At this time, Albert was dating a gorgeous dark-skinned beauty and neighborhood girl Irene M. Irene and Albert were madly in love. When Albert returned on leave from the war, he started frequenting the house of his father's brother, William. William and his wife had seven children, three daughters and four sons. Winnie was the most gorgeous and voluptuous of his cousins, and she was just across the street. Winnie had a white complexion and long hair. Soon the evidence of his frequent visits was visible in Winnie's pregnancy. The belief of colored people at the time was that you take responsibility for and you clean up your mess. Which in plain English means *marry her!* We made fun of this kind of marriage as an MGM marriage (Must Get Married). Was it love? Was it lust? And what role did the politics of color have to play? Winnie was fairer, in fact was white, and Irene was dark. Both were beautiful, both were well-to-do and cultured. The child that was born was Ilene. Albert and Winnie married in 1940 and had two more daughters and a son, Lionel, nicknamed "Nose" because of his signature big family heirloom, his nose.

Soon signs of stress in the marriage started showing. Everyone tried to tell him that Winnie was seeing somebody else, and he never believed it. They both were ridiculed because many regarded their marriage as taboo because they were close family. Both Albert and Winnie grew disillusioned with each other and found alternative comfort. Winnie was always taken around by Mr. X. This and the traumatic experiences of war contributed to Albert's excessive drinking. The marriage between Albert and Winnie was a love-you-hate-you relationship. When Albert had money, the marriage was rosy. When times were hard, Albert would find himself sleeping on a hard place. Winnie would take Albert to court for nonsupport, then Albert would go to jail because Albert always said that he loves Winnie and he would take the money directly to her and not take a receipt and thus had nothing to prove that he had paid maintenance for the children. Eventually Albert didn't have a job so that he couldn't pay maintenance. Again she had him put into jail. I remember on one occasion fetching him at Cape Town station on the Bitterfontein train from de Aar after spending time in prison for six months' hard labor for nonsupport. Albert could not stand on his feet. That night we took sand pebbles and pieces of gravel out of his feet.

Eventually Albert signed on as engineer with Safmarine Shipping Lines and was first on the Edinburgh Castle Passenger Liner and then on the Pendennis Castle Passenger Liner. However, every time, after every voyage, he would come back, and guess what, he would go back to Winnie. No sooner was he with Winnie than the money was up and Winnie would put him out.

Albert only awoke from the nightmare of this marriage in 1963. In March 1963, he jumped ship in Port Elizabeth. He had to go underground as the shipping authorities were looking for him because they were stranded in the harbor. He knew no one in Port Elizabeth. And then he met a beautiful dark-skinned woman, Sarah, who took him in and took him home. Albert lived with Sara in wedded bliss until his death on November 14, 1974. At Albert's funeral, Sarah and Winnie reconciled without forgiving each other for the pain caused in the past.

Albert and Sarah married on April 25, 1963. Out of this marriage, two daughters and a son were born. We lost all contact with him and only realized that something was wrong when the authorities came looking for him at our house. My mom had the belief that he was okay. I do not know why, but she believed that she was going to see him again. And then in 1970, her face lit up as she announced that her brother who was lost will be visiting with us. He came to Cape Town and introduced Sarah, Ursula, Terence, and Althea to us. Albert was accompanied by Hansie, a friend of his, and Hansie's family. They travelled in a Ford Falcon and a Ford Fairlane. My dad at the time had a green Peugeot 403. We accompanied them back to Port Elizabeth—a journey that took us seventeen hours because the Ford Fairlane kept overheating.

Two tragedies struck Albert's family, claiming one child from each marriage. Lionel, who was a manager because he was regarded as white, worked at the Dairy Belle Milk Plant in Epping, Cape Town. Lionel was tragically killed on January 25, 1975, in a motorcar crash during a Saturday afternoon drive around the mountain with Ilene's husband. Ilene was his oldest sister. No one has ever found out what exactly happened in that accident. Lionel was the only child of Albert and Winnie, who moved to Kensington with us in the sixties. My cousin Althea was brutally gunned down in front of her mother, sister, and brother by her husband on January 28, 1995.

Althea came to visit us in Belhar, a suburb of the City of Bellville, at the beginning of 1994. She valued my good opinion of her husband so much that she didn't want to share with me what was going on. She didn't want to taint anybody's image of her husband. They had a childless marriage. However, eventually she broke down and told us about the abusive marriage. She told us how her husband had been treating her badly. He tried to scar her physically because she was so attractive. She was delightfully bright, beautiful and brave. Her radiance earned her the nickname "Sterretjie" (small star). He poured beer on her to let her reek of alcohol she did not drink. He let the dog sleep next to her because he said she's like a dog, and she slept with her pistol under her pillow because he threatened to kill her. She reported him to both station commanders of the different police stations where they worked. She went to psychologists and social workers. She did everything to make everyone aware of what was going on, but nobody did anything because they believed that he was a nice person and exemplary officer. Eventually his service pistol was taken away, but ironically, he stole his station commander's gun on a fishing trip and shot her with it. He got a life sentence. He told her that he would plead temporary insanity because he had only found out very late in life—after being married for many years—that his sister was really his mother and that the woman whom he thought was his mother was in fact his grandmother. He found this out at his grandmother's funeral. He was very jealous of Althea. He used to kick her in the stomach and beat her up and begged the housekeeper not to tell anybody. She was as frail as a scared little girl as she was telling us the story of her married life. She told us about how he would lock her up in the room and go dancing. Because we did not really believe that a man as seemingly delightful and pleasant as her husband could do the things that she was describing, we decided to spend time with them in December of 1994. We stayed with them at their house in Gelvandale for a week and noticed some irregularities. He seemed very disturbed and uncomfortable.

This is how Althea came to the end of her life. It was a scorching hot day in January 1995. Althea's mom, Sarah, older sister Ursula, and brother Terence were sitting, basking in the afternoon sun, eating watermelon in front of the kitchen door, which was on the east side of the house in Gelvandale, Port Elizabeth, in the Eastern Cape Province. They were startled when her husband arrived in a thick coat. He demanded to speak to Althea alone. She was reluctant to accede to his request, uncomfortable and scared. I guess it was logical enough because he had in the past told her that he was going to kill her. He had threatened her and bragged that he would go scot-free because he could plead job stress because he was a police officer. She eventually went inside the house on her mother's insistence that she check on the chops on the stove. As she went inside to check on the meat, he followed her inside at which point she turned around and caught a glimpse of the gun under his coat. She then asked him what he was doing. She continued her walk to the kitchen and the first shot was fired. As she turned around, he just emptied the magazine and walked away. Her mom, brother, and sister witnessed the cold-blooded murder of their sister. The family was frozen with shock. She finally fell out by the door dead. He shot her at one o'clock, and we arrived in Port Elizabeth that same evening. Her blood was still visible at the crime scene. He was a coward and had to shoot her in the back because she was a sharper shooter than he was and he knew it. She had a gun on her and, if given half a chance, would have killed him. At target practice, she always outdid him in shooting the target. She and her mom, brother, and sister saw the gun under his coat. She did not draw first because I guess that she was either hoping that he would not do it or she was frozen in her thoughts with fear of the inevitable.

I was very upset because the family, because of their faith, believed that he should be forgiven and even had him listed as a pallbearer at her funeral. I differed with my aunts and went home to Cape Town and came back for the funeral the next weekend. This was a journey of five hundred miles. I said at the funeral in church, sleep well thou sweet and fair one. Sleep well, Althea, thy strife is o'er. A hush is over Gelvandale for Althea is no more. He was eventually sentenced to life in prison. The pictures that I took at the crime scene were later used at his trial. Althea's funeral was as dignified as her life was beautiful.

Gretel was the daughter of Gretel my grandmother's sister. Mother Gretel died at Gretel's birth. Gretel was fair and very pretty and had a pleasant, sweet and friendly disposition. Gretel married Lloyd. Lloyd was tall and very handsome, with a light-colored complexion. He fought in the same war as Albert. He had four children with Gretel, the eldest of whom drowned at sea. I remember the day we went to lay a wreath at the site of his drowning. I watched in amazement how the wreath glided over the waves. Finally it ended up in a swirl, and it actually disappeared. I remember someone pointing out that that was the exact place where he was last seen before he drowned.

When Lloyd came back from the war, he started having an extramarital affair with my mother's brother-in-law's sister. My mother's brother-in-law was very dark of complexion. This romantic liaison produced a son. Upon the birth of this child,

Lloyd fetched the child and brought him to his wife and forced her to raise him. To Gretel's credit, she raised this son as one of her own.

Lloyd started to abuse and brutalize Gretel. I was witness to many of these beatings, and the feeling of helplessness often left me motionless. It felt that I was going to wet my pants. I would shake in my shoes. I would run away and hide but would also want to stay and see whether I could be of help to Gretel.

I remember on one occasion calling the cops, reporting that a man was making molestations in the street. Annoyingly, the police came to our house demanding to see me, the person who called them to report the molestations. The whole neighborhood knew that I had called the cops. They were stupid in confronting me instead of confronting the man who was disturbing the peace and beating up Gretel.

Lloyd would march up and down the street military style. People in the street feared Lloyd. He was a big strong man. He was rough. He was cruel. He was brutal. He exerted the force of his presence. Lloyd was one of those people who must have suffered some trauma or perhaps posttraumatic stress disorder because before the war, he was the superintendent of the Sunday school and a good father to his children. The effect on his children was visible. I officiated at both Lloyd's and Gretel's funerals. I will never forget the look on Gretel's face during the viewing of his corpse in the coffin. The tears she shed were tears of relief mingled with regret of what might have been. I spoke with her and was surprised that she bore no malice and no fear. She was free at last and could commence the rebuilding of her life in spite of her old age. She grew older gracefully, peacefully, and was endeared by all. She was a real peacemaker. She was the mother of all mothers. No one will ever be able to fathom the depths of her pain, both physically and mentally. She personifies for me the resiliency of the human spirit. I have never ever heard her say a harsh word to or about anybody. Her faith in God held her life together right to the end when she died peacefully. She had the most beautiful, respectful children.

Her children would never cause others pain but the reflection of their own pain.

Another thing to Gretel's credit is that she made me dislike eggs because when I was a child, Gretel sold chickens and eggs to raise money to feed her family because Lloyd had left her and gone to live in Bucksville. Our payment for selling eggs and poultry was half a dozen hard-boiled eggs every Friday night.

My cousin Hillary confused me the most. I met Hillary while we were still living in Vasco. She had a pure white complexion. Hillary and her husband came to visit us in their beautiful lime green left-hand-drive Chevy. Hillary was twenty-two when she found out that she was adopted by my dad's sister, who had a childless marriage. Hillary found this out upon her return from Nyassaland, which today is called Malawi. Hillary was married to Frederick and had two daughters, Faith and Hope. She had what looked like an idyllic marriage. She was always well-dressed, well-mannered, and very refined in her demeanor. When she walked, it was as if she was floating. She had a gracious flowing motion and rhythm in all her movements. She wore pretty free flowing skirts with the most stunning figure belts. She must have had a shoe fetish because her shoes always caught your eye. She captivated you with her easy speaking manner. She related very well to her husband in public. It came as a shock when we received the news that she had left her husband and that she was hanging out with a white guy. She vacated the family mansion and moved into a crummy apartment building. She was always staying in areas that were not nice, appealing, or safe.

Hillary liked to stay in touch with the family periodically. This contact would simply be to inform my mom about her latest whereabouts and about the latest man in her life. She was always telling us about how great the latest guy was that she was dating. She would always tell us about the castles they were building. By the time she called next, she would have changed her boyfriend and may be pregnant again.

She was always aware of her sex appeal. She was always aware of how pretty she was. She was always so trusting, so hopeful, so sweet, so gentle, yet so hurt. I was confused about this angel who was so pained, so distraught at the best of times. Yet she would continue to narrate the fairytale lifestyle. She kept her life going by describing the beautiful life to be. She would describe in the most beautiful language what her house and her family and her children would look like one day.

Only much later in my life did I understand that she was displaying features of abuse in her behavior. She did not grow tired of the marriage and go in search of love. Married life neither satisfied her nor comforted her. It did not ease the pain of her childhood experiences and conflicts. The conflict, however, was in how she deceived herself by pretending to find this love and comfort with white males. The first such male fathered Ally and then he left her, or she left him. And then she went in search of love and Charlie was born. And then she left him or he left her and she went in search of love and Alicia was born.

I will never forget the yearning for love in her eyes. She was affectionate. She was an angel whose wings us lesser mortals could never see. I spoke with Hillary at age seventy-two. She was home alone, taking care of her grandchildren. Her children born in her first marriage have no contact with their mom. They hate her and even when she was sixty told her to find a job and to work. What raw pain must be inside her bosom, yet she pretends to be brave and to say that it does not hurt her. Of course their attitude toward her must hurt, but it is because of her powerlessness to change circumstances that she accepts, not that she has become complacent about her life and lifestyle. Hillary has remained a pleasant, upbeat soul, used and abused by life's events. She still has a song in her heart. She still contacts her family periodically. She still has hopes of a romantic fling with and marriage to a celebrity . . . if only she could meet him, if only he could become aware of her, waiting on him.

Hillary's wasted life continues to haunt me because I know that crimes against children are increasing in intensity and frequency. Children are human, but the world's response to them is often inhumane. Children are physically, emotionally and sexually abused and the justice system is vey lethargic to bring the perpetrators to book. I also know that it is often difficult to convict the abusers because children often lack the verbal skills necessary to convince the court of the crime. Children are such sensory perceivers. Instead of the justice system asking them to state the address where the abuse happened, they should be asked about the colors, the smells, the dog barking, the size of the building and descriptors about the surrounding areas.

Every year more and more children suffer. Often, the children of these children suffer as well. There seems to be a cycle or spiral of abuse. Those things that shape the lives of children when they are small often stay with them and shape them into the adults that go to college, find a job, have children, and govern the country. People who have been pained are often a pain to deal with. They are often high-maintenance personalities who do dumb things in the workplace because the pain base continues to drive them.

I have had to work very hard to confront my own painful memories and do a good job as well. Sometimes these painful memories will be vivid, and at other times, they are vague. They were there, and they influenced my decisions and actions and behavior and interactions and relationships. Sometimes, before I could control it, I may have said a harsh word to someone whom I really would not want to hurt. Sometimes I could be stubborn and stupid by not allowing myself to do the better thing.

Hillary is my constant reminder of the raw deal that children continue to get. In this process, we do forget that these children will one day be in government, deciding over our fate when we are drawing our social pension. I have seen children who were victims of abuse rise above their circumstances and become judges, medical doctors, psychologists, social workers, teachers, and preachers and because I knew their history I could identify how their personal baggage was weighing them down.

I have been a personal witness and often engaged in a dialogue with them as they started doing those same awful things that were done to them. I recall seeing a news report that stated that one in three girls and one in seven boys are victims of abuse annually. In this instance, prevention would surely be preferred to the cure because you cannot undo the harm done; you can only compensate for it.

Many families in South Africa have been scarred by this obsession with color. I can only guess that many countries around the world have similar stories of dysfunction caused in family systems because of the skin color of family members. We do not fully realize how deeply ingrained this color construct is in the mind-set of many. We need a united resolve and action to promote family well-being irrespective of color.

Chapter Six

The Quest for Meaning

Was hilft laufen wenn man nicht auf den rechten Weg ist?[What is the use of running if we are not on the right way?]

German proverb

Walk in the ways of thine heart.

Ecclesiastes 11:19

Let me hasten to say that I have seen the suffering of children, black, white, and colored. Pain is the same across colors, across complexions. Pain is no less painful because you are black or white. I have seen and lived with the suffering of colored children. I have seen the suffering of black children when their parents and family were mercilessly slaughtered. I know the pain of hunger and have seen the desperation on the faces of children who had nowhere to go. And now I have seen the pain and disillusionment of white children and youth and I wonder why we continue to do those things that discourage people to hope and pray for a better day. I have been in houses where tragic death has been an untimely visitor. I have been there when people of color were killed for their convictions. Now I have the guts to question why we cannot put an end to racist classifications and unfair social treatment. I am questioning why we cannot have the same expectations for all children. I am questioning why we cannot give all children an equal chance in life irrespective of race or creed or color.

You may still be wondering why I have been sharing all this traumatic information with you. Life is not just a series of facts that speak for themselves. Facts have to be interpreted and processed. Facts are interpreted truths. We can witness the same event but our perspective or the color of the lenses will ultimately determine our own rendition of the facts. Those events that happened while I was growing up were never self-evident. The interpretation of those events is what was confusing to me. I was the cause of much of my pain. It was the cause of much of my discomfort. It may not have been deterministic in the outcome of my life but is surely associated with those outcomes. I agree that it would be pointless to tell you my story without clarifying what I am either searching for or what it is that I have found and want to share with you.

I came to the workplace in a time of great political unrest and turbulence. There was a mood of uncertainty in the country in the 1990s. It was the onset of the radical transformation period. Rules stating that blacks could not manage whites, for example, were changing. People of color had to learn very quickly how to handle the former oppressors. Sometimes it could be awkward to give instructions to someone who had previously been your boss just because he or she was white.

I came when staff had little or no ambition. This was in no small measure the result of the political turmoil at the time. Bombings and cases of "terrorism" were rife. Everyone was suspicious of everyone. Fear had gripped the nation. Whether we want to admit it or not, the political party that governs has a profound impact on the culture and climate within our organizations.

After all these conflicting images of and during childhood, we have to find a job. May I remind you that for some unfortunate ones, the nightmare just does not stop, not ever. I know children who grew up in this conflict, exposed to alcohol and drug abuse, dysfunctional families, broken homes, fractured environments, and other disruptive experiences. They went on to marry spouses with similar experiences, just ensuring more of the same. They became victims of domestic violence, spousal abuse, poverty, and disillusionment. They stayed in those abusive marriages because, like my friend Alicia, they believed that it is the right thing to do. Alicia was a high-performing professional who was married to a noted gynecologist. I often asked her why she was staying, in spite of the bruises to her body and the fabrication of lies to rationalize the cause of the bruises. My jaw dropped one day when she just blurted it out informing me that her dad, an equally renowned professional, was constantly beating up her mom.

We have to put on a brave face and go to work. We bring diverse motivations, needs, expectations, experiences, and learning styles to the organization. By the time we get to the workplace we have all been rejected in some way shape or form. Employees in the workplace often feel isolated, targeted, lonely, angry, and unmotivated, and they often have to mask their true feelings. Do you still remember that world-shattering first breakup with your boyfriend or girlfriend at high school, for some even as early as elementary school? We respond to these challenges, and eventually, we have a habitual response even if the personalities are different, but the stimulus is the same. This learned behavior or pattern makes objective evaluation of behavior almost impossible. Add to this the different child-rearing patterns and diverse cultural practices and you have a perfect mask for authentic organizational behavior. How can the observation, analysis, or diagnosis of organizational behavior be precise if the participants are pretending, are masking, are hiding their real needs? Pretence prevents staff from relaxing. Office staff become like a woman who has been on high stiletto heels all day who wants to get home to kick off her shoes and relax, but cannot. They have to perform in spite of their discomfort with who they really are and what they are experiencing in the moment. This fairly regularly leads to office affairs, gossip in the workplace, and the troubles these phenomena lead to. Alternatively, staff may be so unhappy in themselves that this contributes to their underperformance and the making of mistakes. A quick strategy is to blame others for one's incompetence. However, blaming others robs you of energy; eventually you will be absent in your presence, fatigued by your own devices and constant defeats. I suggest that we reimagine work life.

We often cannot undo our experience or erase our history. Our history becomes the narrative that keeps sense of who we are alive. Our lives have to have meaning and purpose in order for us to be gainfully employed and truly engaged in the workplace. In the event that we cannot cancel what happened to us, we can learn the art of reframing and repositioning ourselves, our lifestyle and our journey. Reframing gives you the opportunity to change your perspective, evaluation and disposition. Changing your attitude when you can change nothing else might sometimes be the only thing that you have power to do. I believe that perception determines interaction. If you frame yourself as incapable, powerless, and in a corner with no escape, you probably will be trapped forever. The mind is powerful. Once again I will draw a metaphor from my work with children and young people who were victims of sexual, physical and/or emotional abuse. There was nothing they could do to undo the harm done to them, a harm caused by others. But these survivors can and do reposition themselves not as vulnerable recipients of the harm by performing to their strengths and their assets. They can be helped to find ways to compensate for and to rework and renegotiate the harm. Their biggest enemy is developing a victim mentality because if you think that you are doomed, you are. You can also reposition yourself by physically taking yourself out of harm's way. If you are orphaned by AIDS, you can be lonely and alone. However, if you reframe and reposition yourself as loveable and able to receive love, care and concern, you can allow yourself to be embraced. I do believe that perception determines interaction.

Hatred can thus be imagined and dealt with, not as a force separate from love, but as love in its frustrated, negative form. Anxiety can be imagined and dealt with as love threatened from within the relationship. Jealousy can be imagined and dealt with as love threatened from outside the relationship. Loneliness can be imagined and dealt with as love which cannot find its object. Grief can be imagined and dealt with as love that has had its object and lost it. Despair can be imagined and dealt with as love that has been rejected and made to feel unlovable. Togetherness, belongingness, a warm sense of well-being, a mellow mood of joy—these are imagined as love fulfilled and it is possible.

Do you know who you are and what you are living for? Do you know what your highest calling in life is? Do you know what it is that you really want out of life? The way you respond to these questions reflects how you experience the world. Many people I have worked with and have asked these questions admitted that unless they were sure who they were, it was indeed difficult to be satisfied. My contention has always been that I do not work for an organization. I *am* the organization. I *am* the work. Often I am the only interface between the organization and the clients, customer or other stakeholders. Who I am is depicted in my demeanor, my attitude, my disposition. It plays out in the way I dress and the way I engage with people.

I salute organizations that spend vast amounts of resources on staff training and professional development. However, staff often has a need for therapy and not just training. Training in my view is not to be framed as an "add on" but rather as an "add in" to staff's repertoire of skills. Staff has to discover their skill sets from within. Adding on the skills of another often makes one clumsy. You cannot engage in battle with another's armor. Training should not be viewed as appendage to organizational life. Training is essential. It should be a core organizational value.

April 27, 1994, was indeed a golden day in the history of the South African rainbow nation. I can remember the bright sunny day in a long line of people waiting to cast their vote for the first time. The euphoria and proverbial smell of the pot of gold at the end of the rainbow were the stuff that fairytales are made of. We were all feeling a new spring to our steps. We were floating on the promises of the ANC. This great day heralded the onset of the democratization of our country and ushered in the institutionalization of a human rights culture where there is a need for strong and healthy functioning organizations to reinforce this new way of life. The ultimate goal and promise of the struggle for freedom kept the flame of hope ablaze.

Yet many people are now wallowing in despair, simply because organizations have not designed the strategies or built the capacity that will allow them to adapt to the demands of the new political dispensation. In 2009 and the third election, we are seeing the report card of efforts to build the new South Africa. Crime is still a huge problem. Matriculation rates are still a big problem. If we do not have strong institutions from justice to education, from culture to economics, and from sport to housing, we cannot succeed with nation building. It must be clear by now that power politics today are having the same effect as the power politics of the old regime, which ruled by driving the fear of God into us. Now the fear of the ANC and its own brand of power politics is being driven into us. You can understand how power politics have stifled organizational development by reinforcing a false sense of security. Many organizations on both sides of the political spectrum are now finding that the "wheels" of the organization are coming off.

My concern here is for those organizations that are serving the needs of the people through housing, juvenile justice, schools, and the multifarious needs of the poor. With the downturn in the economy, worldwide, social needs will increase. It is becoming a struggle to continue to celebrate a brief joy that now seems to elude and frustrate the masses. In spite of this glorious new post-apartheid time, South Africa is still very unfinished, politically speaking. The political terrain seems to be foreign, rough and uncomfortable, threatening and challenging for people who want to participate in the political processes because they have needs and aspirations and they need help. The human services organizations, for example, that are supposed to render those services are often found wanting and are not firmly embedded in the new political dispensation. The radical change of the political dispensation that had been paid for with limbs, loss of life and emotional pain, seems to demand changes that were either not anticipated or simply ignored. The political system does not seem to be in synchronization with the needs of all the groups, both minority and majority, yet. We also are witnessing a range of unintended consequences of our political actions. I am convinced that the ANC did not set out to bring mayhem to the country. I am sure that they do not want to be seen as "doing to them what they did to us" in the new South Africa. I am sure that the ANC never intended to play power politics and cause pain in the lives of the citizens of South Africa. If the adults in power cannot control or help themselves, then they must get help because what the country needs is whole and healed people to govern with fairness and justice for all. We need to create a South Africa that is worth living in for all of its citizens, including its children and young people. South Africa does not have to fear a continuing brain drain. People will be prepared to defend their country if they really know and feel that they are valued in their country of birth. People will be proud to be South African if we can only stop making our country a fool's paradise. Let our leaders stop their political bickering. Let our leaders lead by example. Let our leaders set the moral compass and tone for the country and it will not be long before every citizen will follow the example of those leaders.

On the other hand, there are still too many people in the dark about politics and about becoming adept at participating in the political system. It is indeed very dark, and the darkness seems to incapacitate the country and its organizations and institutions. However what we perceive this darkness to be is of vital importance. We can either perceive it as the darkness of a cave or that of a tunnel. One very striking commonality between a cave and a tunnel is the darkness. It is indeed very dark on the political economic and social horizons. What this darkness is, is actually a leadership challenge. If we are merely managing the darkness because we perceive it to be a cave, we will only succeed in maintaining the status quo. Surviving in the cave is a management challenge. If the darkness is perceived it to be that of a tunnel, we will design change strategies that will assist us in negotiating our way forward, out of the tunnel, and that is leadership. Forging our way through the tunnel is a leadership challenge. Hiding in the cave will give us a false sense of security but will not get us anywhere.

If many of the citizens have been in a political cave for the past fifteen years, their minds are programmed differently than those who are participating in the political processes. It is time for open and honest dialogue between those who have withdrawn from the political processes and those who are driving the political processes. We need to evaluate what is really going on in the country. We need to embrace a future that is worthwhile for all the citizens in a nonracial society. We need to say to each other that everything is going to be okay, and then make it so.

There is a similar trajectory between global warming and the harshness of life faced by children, youth, and families in South Africa, and unless something real is done to reverse trends, the consequences will continue to be disastrous. There will be a point of no return when the mounting impact of poor social conditions will take people over the edge. People over time can only suffer so much and no more. Suffering people will reach saturation point sometime during this century. If the trend of abuse is not reversed, then reaching that suffering saturation point will be irreversible. There is a real global warning that if we do not do for at-risk children, youth, and families what they need, the world will continue to hemorrhage and lose valuable, promising lives, and with that, the future is bleak. Do we really know what is happening to children and young people in our communities? What do you know about at-risk young people, people in foster care, in residential care, in independent living, and for children aging out of the system? Think about children who have nothing and *do not even know that they can want something*, children whose courage is being denied. Think about a culture of hopelessness. Think of family systems of hopelessness. Now think of successive family systems of hopelessness. Think about what we may learn from a study of the psychology of hopelessness. Think about children who have become relationship-wary, unable to trust. Think about children who are estranged from their kith and kin and their home environment, and even alienated from who they really are, children for whom denial and the delusion of indulgence is the best safe space and hope for survival. I know these families and children who do not have anything, who never had anything and are probably resigning themselves to the thought of never having anything. I know the glazed look. I know the how hungry they become for attention and even the smallest token gesture produces a smile a Nile wide. When one or even a couple of people experience this hopelessness, they may get some encouragement from their peers, relatives, or friends. However, when a society or group manifest this hopelessness, who can they turn to? When will this abuse and waste of human lives ever end?

It is time for citizens to take their country back. It is time for every citizen to become an active participant in the political processes of their country. It is time for every South African to participate in elections. It is time for every citizen to hold the feet of their elected representatives to the fire, figuratively. It is imperative that we hold our elected officials accountable. South Africa can be a model nation. A dynamic South African renaissance depends on the active participation of every citizen of the beloved rainbow nation.

I believe that many of us are blessed to go through this life twice. The first time we are active participants in even those events over which we have no control. Our lives are subject to and part of the history that is being made. We roll along, never questioning why what is happening, is happening. We are mere cogs and spokes in the wheel of time. But then, there comes a moment when your eyes are opened and you do more than see, you comprehend, you question, you become involved in shaping history, even though there may still be things that you still do not understand; but you do what you can. You do everything you can in that moment when you arrive at the crossroads where you can no longer leave things as they are. Not everyone realizes that life has meaning and purpose. Not everyone knows what they are living for or what their highest calling in life is. You realize that your life has meaning and purpose. You make the difference, so help me God, you cannot stay the same and exit this life and take up residence in your grandest bedroom ever, your coffin. You cannot rest in peace until you find the purpose and niche especially for you; because only you can do what you do best. You and your skills and resources are needed because we need to build community in neighborhoods. Healthy relationships are essential in building community in your neighborhood.

Many people live in neighborhoods that they like. Many people live in neighborhoods that they do not like. Many people live in neighborhoods for which they have an "I don't care" attitude. Many people do care about their neighborhoods. In today's chilling economic climate most people will have to live in neighborhoods because they have no other choice. People who pass by neighborhoods are quick to give them a label. Often these labels of the neighborhood mirror the stereotype firmly etched in the mind-set of the passerby. Some people who live in neighborhoods love the label, especially if it matches the name of their sports car and adds to their prestige. Some people who live in neighborhoods hate the label because it matches their empty wallets and add to their misery. If you live in the ghetto, have no money, and have loud and violent neighbors the constant fear might put a cap on the pleasantness of your life. There is not much to get excited about if you live in a neighborhood where all the residents are equally poor and have to eke out an existence.

We need to remind ourselves that people, human beings, parents and children live in these neighborhoods, no matter the location and conditions in the neighborhood. These mothers love their babies no less than any other mammas. These dads like to play with their children no less than any other dads. However, it can sometimes be difficult to juggle your needs and wants. It can be difficult to hold down three jobs and to make time for your family, nurture your ego, and accomplish things you can be proud of. Some neighborhoods are doing well. They are peaceful, beautiful, and quiet. Other neighborhoods are boisterous and ugly, and there is nothing inviting or exciting about them. I like to think of these neighborhoods that are so scary to passersby as neighborhoods of no lesser value. A flatline or inactivity, on either an electrocardiogram or an electroencephalogram, signifies the death of a human being. I believe that unlike human beings who have only one lifetime, neighborhoods have multiple lifetimes. However a particular neighborhood can go through phases of well-being, degradation, or being a flatline neighborhood. A flatline neighborhood occurs when the risk factors in a neighborhood annihilate the protective, positive elements. Crime, abuse, domestic violence, drug abuse, alcohol abuse, unemployment, and inadequate infrastructure and resources will exacerbate the impact of the risk factors and eventually result in a flatline neighborhood.

We need to build community in our neighborhoods because we will no longer be pallbearers of the casket containing the last remains of our neighborhood. We will be torchbearers of the reconstruction and redevelopment of our neighborhood. We need an epidemic of camaraderie, goodwill, and good neighborliness. We need to help our children find their way before they get lost in the quagmire created by the compounding effect of the risk factors in the neighborhood. We need to engage our young people before they engage in activities that put themselves and their neighborhoods at risk. We need to help our young adults embrace a vision and mission that will impact the quality of life of everyone in the neighborhood. We need to help our young people establish, nurture, and maintain healthy, growth-producing relationships. We need to connect our older adults, our grandparents, with valuable and dignified opportunities to continue serving community-building efforts in neighborhoods. Our grandparents can engage in arts and crafts, reading and storytelling to incapacitated children, young people and adults. Why not mobilize a multigenerational team to paint a mural in a pediatric ward of a hospital or community hall?

How about starting with rejuvenated activities at our neighborhood, halls, parks, libraries, and pools? How about bringing fun back into our neighborhoods? How about making it safe for children to play outside? How about arranging community events like a car wash, a barbeque, a dance party, or a community cleanup?

The hostile forces of this chilling economy will leave us no option but to reinvent cost-saving activities. Organize some block parties, swop and shop exchanges and other communal exchange of resources. Activate the community. Whereas Community Redevelopment Agencies (CRA) develops the physical aspects of the community, the people need to align the mind-set in the community to match the CRA projects. Communities need to own the redevelopment.

This economy has made a radical difference to our shopping habits. We used to go to the grocery store with a pocket full of dollars and we bought a cart full of groceries. Now, however, we go with a cart full of pennies, and we only get a pocket full of groceries. Neighborhoods can be redeveloped and the spirit of people can be rekindled. You do not always need big budgets to achieve big things. Often the most profound change is wrought by the little courtesies in life.

I have worked with children, young people, and families who were living in a sewer in Retreat, a suburb of Cape Town. I have worked with children who lived in a forty-five-gallon drum. I have worked with young people who were homeless. Flatline neighborhoods can change. In flatline neighborhoods in South Africa, America, and around the world where there are almost no protective factors and almost no sense of community, those elements that can bring back life should be put in place. We need neighborhoods that are safe, healthy, vibrant and growth-producing. Flatline neighborhoods will come to life again when the risk factors are minimized. Policymakers, researchers, politicians, and civic leaders have a responsibility to lead rebuilding efforts in their neighborhoods. Flatline neighborhoods must have proper infrastructure and resources. Far too many flatline neighborhoods are still without accessible schools, libraries and healthcare resources. Governments should not wait until people in flatline neighborhoods start to protest and revolt because there is a tipping point when people will say enough. How much further will you and I allow this exploitation of people to continue just because they are poor, and their color is not the same as ours, and they speak a different language?

All people in flatline neighborhoods need to know that we are all working together to cocreate a community worth living in for all in our neighborhood. The workplace is a special place where we can reconstruct our communities. We spend at least a third of our day at work. Why not spend it not only productively but also meaningfully? I have tried to create a model that can celebrate and convey meaning and purpose even in the workplace. Who said that working cannot be fun, joyous and passionate?

We will indeed know that meaningfulness has returned to life when we do for others what they need and not just what we want to. Life will have meaning when we can all enjoy the good things in life. We should all be able to enjoy a ball game, the smell of flowers, national parks, amusement parks, family outings, sunsets, freedom to worship, and participation in free and fair elections.

The meaning of life should be a nonnegotiable value in life. Meaning should be a virtue. The meaning to life should be the umbrella that protects everyone from the vulnerability to and exploitation by others based on an ideology that favors people on the basis of race, creed and color. Without meaning, we will all stagnate at one point or another. Meaningfulness will be reinforced when we can all engage in service learning, corporate social responsibility, boys and girls clubs, big brothers, big sisters, and other worthwhile causes. Instead of long discussions and cheap talk about meaning, let us do something that will be meaningful. Will you? Will you?

Chapter Seven

The Post-Apartheid Organizational Framework

The majority of South Africans, black and white, recognize that apartheid has no future. It has to be ended by our own decisive mass action in order to build peace and security. The mass campaign of defiance and other actions of our organization and people can only culminate in the establishment of democracy. There must be an end to white monopoly on political power, and a fundamental restructuring of our political and economic systems to ensure that the inequalities of apartheid are addressed and our society thoroughly democratized.

—Nelson Mandela (1918-   )

Let me introduce you to a model that was born out of my experience in the workplace.

Organizabonding

Mission

Expand Comprehensive Organizational Capacity with a Diverse Workforce Through Effective Human Capital Management for All.

Vision

Cocreating a Work Milieu Worth Working in for All.

1. Prolegomena

> *An organization has a mission, purpose, and reason for being. It is people who personify the organizational promise and purpose. As such, human relations in an organization is a highly complex and multifaceted phenomenon within which an almost unimaginable number of policies, methodologies, strategies, ideologies, politics, and bureaucracies interplay. The challenge is to energize the individual mind-set, transcend the comfort zone, liberate the new collective mind-set, and work together as a team to make the impact on the bottom line beneficial to all. The increasingly heterogeneous work milieu, where employees bring their own values, cultures, traditions, methods of interacting and communicating, and worldviews to the workplace can be challenging. The challenge then is to cocreate a lifestyle that is meaningful for all in a diverse workplace.*

Allow me to pay homage to my parents who inspired this search to contribute to the meaningfulness of organizational life. Something that my late mama said: you cannot build lasting joy on the tears that you cause others. Stepping on others is painful for them. The pain that you cause others will certainly revisit you.

She also advised me not to catch a falling knife. How we respond in and to a crisis is crucial. My late daddy said: You can force your way through a crowd but you cannot force yourself into the heart of one individual. He also told me so many stories about the importance of attitude that I include when I do training and professional development. One story was about a woman in the village whose mother-in-law was treating her very badly. In her excruciating pain and utter frustration she went to the sangoma for advice. After listening to her story, he mixed a potion and instructed her to use just a little bit in her mother-in-law's food every day. He said that because she knew that this poison would finally lead to the death of her mother-in-law that she should be as nice as possible because she did not want people to point a finger at her upon the death of her mom-in-law. This went on for months, and eventually, her mother-in-law was telling the villagers how nice her daughter-in-law was. The relationship between the woman and her mother-in-law improved to such an extent that she went back to the sangoma, pleading with him for a potion that can reverse the imminent death of her mother-in-law. The sangoma said that she should not worry because he only mixed a potion that would make her mother-in-law healthier. He just wanted her to change her attitude in spite of her mother-in-law's bad attitude toward her. Then my dad told me about the parishioner who told his pastor that he would no longer be attending church services because all the people in the church were just hypocrites. The man was a pig farmer. One Saturday the pastor went to the farm to visit. On his way out, he offered to buy one of the pigs from the farmer. The farmer showed him his prized piglets. The pastor noticed one with six legs and offered to buy it. The farmer said that the pastor could have it for free. As the pastor was leaving with the piglet under his arm, the farmer wanted to know exactly why the pastor wanted the crippled pig. The pastor said that he was going to show all the people what kind of pig farmer the farmer was. The farmer protested by saying that that was not true. The pastor said that that was exactly what the farmer was saying about his parish just because there were one or two hypocrites in his church.

My parents have made me realize that my identity is not just about who I am; it is about whose I am in the universe. My sense of belonging and engagement energizes my commitment. This then drives me to organize the bonding, the belonging of workers in the workplace that is striving for the best interests of the collective and not just that of the boss and the shareholders.

The workplace can be a battle zone of the mind, body and spirit. The resultant friction is often caused by a disconnected, fragmented workforce. When workers are only symbolically involved and not authentically engaged, the sparks tend to fly frequently. The workplace often does not define engagement. Engagement at its best implies mutuality, a taking up of responsibility; each for the other. Engagement is the response to an invitation to take up this responsibility. Engagement implies a willingness to share, care and to be obviously motivated and committed to a longer term process. Engagement is not an exercise in semantics nor is it playing around with words. Engagement is not just talk about community, involvement, commitment, belonging and togetherness. Engagement can mean different things to different people because people from a high context culture may view engagement different to people from a low context culture. One can put it more simply by saying that because people's world view may differ; their take on engagement may differ. Engagement can be conceptualized and defined as having the following essential components:

> Engagement is accepting the invitation (reciprocal action) to take up responsibility for each other (commitment) en route to the concretization (rationale) of the organizational mission and goals. (results)

The workplace needs to embrace mutuality in place of a winner takes all mentality for that can be destructive. Co-workers as well as supervisors need to actively take up responsibility for each other. I do not see this mutuality in our corporate culture and learning community. I sometimes see a win and trample at all costs as long as the supervisor has all the power. I sometimes see a military style engagement that is nothing but hostile.

The workplace needs to be conceptualized and set up as a caring, being concerned about, and growing each other comprehensive mindset and culture. This will ensure that every worker will be committed to quality standards of practice. The maxim should be "engagement by all for all". No worker should be disconnected or disengaged in the workplace. Every worker should be empowered. The issues and frustrations of disgruntled workers should be dealt with. If workers are not engaged any one can be a tragedy waiting to happen. The maxim is to hold your engaged workers close and your disengaged workers, closer. We are living in an era when tragedies in the workplace are increasing. We place our workforce at risk when we ignore those workers who are dissatisfied. The agenda of these workers may eventually sabotage the organizational mission. There is an added responsibility for supervisors to embrace diversity and to embrace those staff members who are very easy to ignore and frustrate simply because these workers are not mainstream or conventional. It is relatively easy for a disengaged worker to handicap organizational progress. Engagement is most vibrant when it is the product of the organizational diversity policy.

I come from a high context culture where we were all engaged under the aegis of ubuntu. Ubuntu means, a person is a person through other persons. Ghandi believed that this concept could transform western civilizations. Ubuntu has to do with what it means to be truly human. Ubuntu means that we are inextricably woven into the joy and challenges of others. Ubuntu is essential to life. It speaks about our belonging, our mutuality. Ubuntu establishes community. We have authentic community when we all have a voice. Community implies sharing and involvement in communal values and co-creative activities as well as interaction in multiple contexts. Bad interpersonal relationships and a lack of communication skills often bedevil the striving for community. We lack quality in our communal interaction because we either do not engage authentically or we do not take ownership for our relationships. Remember that there is no joy without a challenge. Ubuntu is the essence of being human. It speaks of the fact that my humanity is caught up and is inextricably bound up in yours. I am human because I belong. It speaks about wholeness, it speaks about compassion. A person with ubuntu is open and available to others. This willingness to grow in tandem and to co-create, innovate and renew will be evidenced by some or all of the following attributes:

- Welcoming and inclusive,
- Wholeness and hospitability,
- Warmth and generosity,
- Willingness to share with others,
- Willingness to be vulnerable and to give recognition to the efforts of others,
- Will not feel threatened by the ability and goodness of others,
- Will do no harm to others because harm done to others is harm done to self.
- Putting others down is sinking yourself.

Organizabonding promotes this all embracing culture that is welcoming and willing to take smart risks. This workplace culture is less punitive and more rewarding not just in monetary terms but in acknowledging and giving recognition to the achievements and contributions of others.

Directing, leading and the administration of an organization is risk and reward intensive. Leaders, managers, supervisors and administrators should realize that there is a more expedient way of conducting the business. You do not always have to be in control. You do not have to instill the fear of God into your coworkers and subordinates. You do not have to pull rank and flaunt your powerful position in order to motivate people to energize and execute the organizational mission. You can achieve the same or even better results by engaging in the principles of remediation employment practice. In the remediation employment practice the quest is to help the worker master the skills needed to execute the tasks, roles and responsibilities. The worker does not get penalized for inability but would rather get both management and moral support. Termination of services is never a first threat. We live in a democratic country and the *audi alteram partem* rule should always be upheld. This rule simply means that the other party has a right to be heard. If you care, then show it in the way you interact with coworkers.

It is important that learning managers understand the need for workers to have a sense of membership, belonging and ownership in an organization. Not enough is done in organizations to work on the mutuality among the CEO, managers, and staff. The *Organizabonding* and relational education model of teaching and learning is a system of interactive skills training and technical assistance workshops. It seeks to mentor management and provide support to directors, principals, teachers, and staff and direct care workers, and make a meaningful difference in organizations, institutions, schools and in the lives of children, young people, and families. This model is more than managing daily process complexities, more than doing "stuff" right, more than boosting sales; it is about managing human relations, cocreating synergy and a team commitment to service excellence. This model has life-changing potential because it is an encounter, dealing effectively with managed confrontation, difference, and conflict. *Organizabonding* is a workforce development instrument. *Organizabonding* is an organizational philosophy that grew from experience, not just theory. Organizabonding creates buy-in by the workforce that promotes a sense of belonging in the project. Input and output of staff is impacted by their sense of belonging within an organizational system

Organizabonding was spawned as both assessment of and response to the challenges faced by organizations when South African civil society transformed from the apartheid ideology to embrace democratic principles as it strived to usher in a new political dispensation and a basic human rights culture for all.

Many trends and factors contributed to the complexity of this transition. I was told by my supervisor that I have to stand behind workers to ensure that they perform. I was told that they won't do a good job unless they are being watched. One had to crack the whip, proverbially speaking. This was puzzling to me because I experienced this differently. I knew of many people like myself who had a good work ethic and who were performing beyond expectations. Power, force, coercion, position, and status were the order of the day during apartheid rule. Organizational life often mimicked the contemporary political will (or lack thereof). The only way workers could respond was through covert operations that undermined the productivity levels in organizations. Passive aggression was a well-utilized tool.

When Nelson Mandela became the first democratically elected black president of South Africa in 1994, I realized that for the new South Africa to emerge, we would have to transcend our differences, utilize our creativity and join resources in our best efforts to rebuild the nation. However, we were entering an ahistorical period. This time period is unrelated to history, past models, and traditions, and we could not feed on the stereotypes of the past. A new and unique era was emerging.

Now more than ever, we needed a commitment to professional standards and human relations based on mutual respect. At first we were all reluctant to leave our culturally sanctioned comfort zones behind us. We were all rather defensive. However, we needed everyone's input in order to respond authentically to what it was that we had to do as well as make our togetherness meaningful. We discovered that the workforce needed therapy, not training, in order to deliver on the organizational mission.

Organizations are often unproductive because of conflicted interpersonal or human relations in the workplace. Senior management is often a causal factor because their management style and skills do not synchronize with the often younger collective mind-set of the staff team. Senior management often "cap" the potential of subordinates and this is frustrating. Also, management does not always know the challenges presented by today's customers/clients.

Many studies reference problems in organizations because of "how" management staff is recruited and appointed. I have found that the biggest problem begins when organizations transition from one director to the next, in particular the critical moment when the new boss or supervisor "takes over" and inherits the situation, baggage, script, and all. *Organizabonding* takes care of the potential transition period problems. It is a model that ensures that there is membership or a sense of belonging and ownership. There is the need to overcome the distrust or hostility created by the change and how it was handled (or not handled). This is also the time for the new director to be adept at using those skills to win friends and influence people and to enhance organizational synergy through compatibility, reconciliation, and relationships. You can look back over your career and will be able to identify people and the difference they made to the organization, both good and bad. This I think is the crux of our work in leading change. What is modeled both vertically and horizontally is crucial to succession planning in the organization.

The most important concern is that the workforce does not realize that professional workplace relations happen en route to *self*. The same holds true with clients; working relationally with others is in fact a confrontation with self. Self-knowledge is key. If you have not mastered yourself, how can you engage in relations with others without trying to control them or to blame them for everything that goes wrong in your own life?

If you cannot manage your relationship with your customers, you cannot measure it either. Likewise if you cannot measure your relationship with your customers, you cannot manage it effectively. Customer relationship management and marketing strategies are essential for the sustainability of the organization, as well as for beneficial outcomes. This is a brilliant segue for developing a corporate citizenship agenda and can so easily unite the team. If you can unite your team by focusing on a cause, they can all support like building houses for homeless people or supporting a children's hospital or doing an environmentally friendly green project.

Although change is not linear and sequential, the key moments in the Organizabonding process are sequential for obvious reasons. I will engage in a dialogue with the CEO or departmental leader and do a SWOT analysis of the CEO or leader. The focus of this exploratory dialogue is to uncover the CEO's personal and professional vision and goals and how this relates to the needs within the organizational system and structure. The CEO will fill out a questionnaire. Once I have this, I administer the same questionnaire with the staff. I then structure the three-day intensive interactive training.

I have spent more than twenty years working with dysfunctional young people, families, and human services organizations. All this training is based on my master's and doctoral research into human services organizations in South Africa, where I was the director in Human Services in the Western Cape Province. (Please feel free to "Google" me to see where I have worked and conducted training at http://www.cultureal.com.)

Research indicates that there is a direct correlation between organizational climate and culture and the level of productivity of staff. Staff members impact the quality of services delivered by agencies in the human services sector. Staff members bring diverse motivations, needs, expectations, experiences, and learning styles to the organization. The orienting response reinforcement pattern makes objective evaluation of behavior almost impossible. Add to this, the diverse child-rearing patterns and cultural practices and you have a perfect mask for authentic organizational behavior. Often the interpersonal (and sometimes the intrapersonal) challenges and issues of staff get in the way of the organizational needs and mission. It is said in Africa that when two elephants struggle, the grass suffers. Likewise, when two strong personalities clash, others are often hurt in the process. Staff may become disillusioned and bitter. Bitterness is the atmosphere produced within when we meditate over life's circumstances and decide that we have been given an unfair deal. Such bitterness simply makes staff bite the bullet and not want to become better at their tasks, roles and responsibilities. Alternatively we fail to realize that blaming others robs you of your energy. Eventually, as I have said, you will be absent in your presence, fatigued by your own devices and constant defeats. We sometimes want to run, but we cannot hide because that which we are so anxious to conceal we actually, casually, reveal. Past experiences in life create a perception activated survival trigger (PAST) that lulls people in their comfort zones. They continue with the delusion of indulgence that interferes with their reflection of reality and they actually become stubbornly defensive.

We all need to make sure that the halo of our professional arrogance does not dim the radiance of our humaneness. We dare not forget that our customers, clients, and stakeholders are human too. We also need to remind ourselves that if people do not get what they need, they take what they want anyway, anyhow.

The issues and challenges I describe here can be managed effectively through transitioning of paradigm shifts, mind-set changes; skill sets training, self-awareness, awareness of learning styles, cultural diversity and competency, team building, and getting the right persons to do the job, among others.

2. Principles

Organizabonding is a different way of engaging key participants. The trainer acts as host and teaches participants the skills of hosting protocols, persons, policies and procedures. The idea is to explore, to dialogue, to cocreate synergy. Working relationally is the challenge. Working relationally is about extending and accepting the invitation to take up responsibility for each other. The decision and right to make the choice is inalienable to everyone involved in this process. In the twenty-first-century world with its oversupply of choices, working relationally is not about prescribing what to choose but rather to teach and model those skills needed to make the right decision, the right choice. Understanding and respecting the lived reality of the other person as authentic is essential to the cocreation of meaning. One cannot make an informed decision about people by just observing what they eat or what they wear. One has to know and understand their lifestyle and the rationale for that lifestyle because learning about a lifestyle and creating the personal lifestyle happens at the same time. One has to learn to walk in another's shoes while remaining open to learning because working relationally is about reeducation. Relational education is not about the mastery of abstract knowledge, skills, and attitudes only. It is, more importantly, about the practical mastery of the "achievements" of everyday life. Effort is rewarded and celebrated more than achievement.

My three-day workshop is aimed at training staff in the skill sets that will enhance positive interpersonal relations: the foundation of teamwork and synergy. Teamwork is key in interactions with others, staff, and customers. Staff will be adept at dealing with workplace challenges and crises. A renewed commitment to a shared organizational vision and quality service delivery is the goal. This shared vision then becomes an authentic vision and not just symbolic activity.

The workforce needs to have a sense of belonging and meaning while engaging in protocols and activities within the organization. Without this meaningfulness, it will indeed be complicated to achieve the goals set by the organization. Likewise, it would be difficult to develop an organizational culture of belonging, ownership and quality that is conducive to service delivery and learning outcomes where there is no match between individual needs and goals and organizational needs and goals.

Often staff members do not fail to perform; instead, the organization performs in such a way that staffs fail. A dysfunctional workplace does not boost staff morale. In the school system, for example, teachers may be teaching to the state's comprehensive testing system because it is driving the educational occurrences and processes. However, until the value of relational education as an educational philosophy and applied practice is understood and implemented by administrators and educators, in fact by every person who may influence learners and learning outcomes, we will not have an educational system, but mere components or parts of a dysfunctional system; outcomes will be unsatisfactory. Albert Einstein stated that not everything that can be counted counts; and not everything that counts can be counted.

The relational education model of teaching and learning is relationship dependent. In talking about the identity of a child we know that more important than who I am is "whose" I am. A mother may carry a child for nine months during the pregnancy but may not care for the child once the child is born, The child knows whose he or she is by who claims responsibility for the child and this is crucial for the child in terms of his or her identity. Sometimes no one at home or in the primary system takes responsibility for a child. The quality of this relationship or taking up responsibility the each for the other, between educator and learner or student in the learning process, makes the teaching effective. The real meaning or truth is engineered through the cocreative dialogue between teacher and learner. In this manner relational education engineers a learning environment that is liberating and growth producing. Even failure is understood as a necessary step toward success. "Tuning in" to where management and staff are at is more important than speeding up the management and staff to "get it."

3. Process

The following sequential synopsis will help you form a conceptual framework of this leadership and organizational capability and capacity building, education, training and technical assistance model facilitating the comprehensive management of the human capital investment in human services organizations. *Ideally, Organizabonding is a thirty-day process.* The actual training takes place over three days. You want to give participants time to reflect, report, and relearn. The training can however be customized to fit your schedule.

One of the evenings could be used for social interaction, recognition, and organizational storytelling.

a. The first step is to enter into an exploratory dialogue with you, the president, CEO, regional or department director. You will spell out your vision and deliver your organizational SWOT analysis, culminating in your five-year strategic plan for the organization. You will also give a brief overview of your personal and professional goals and frustrations. You will do a personality-type assessment.
b. The second step is to send me a job description for everyone who will be involved in the capability and capacity building training.
c. The third step is to inform staff that you have contracted with me and that they will receive a questionnaire from me to assess organizational culture and climate.

Based on this feedback, the training is then customized and presented and facilitated over three days.

A personal workbook for each participant is prepared. The organizational logo is on the cover of the training manuals. Handouts are given to complement work covered during training.

The interactive workshop starts with a Myers-Briggs Type Inventory, stories, metaphors, and role-playing that help staff understand and confront themselves through introspection and self-awareness. The final day has a laser focus on organizational mission and outcomes.

On day one, a Myers Briggs Type Inventory is administered. We may also use a FIRO-B or any other relevant test that will describe interaction, learning styles and preference. Staff members are equipped to construct a collage of their personal and professional lives. Self-reflection is essential in these exercises.

As you will see, *this is a thirty-day process* of which the three-day or customized training is part of the comprehensive plan. You will hopefully for the first time have a useful barometer of the quality of interactive-intensive engagement among staff, management and clients. You will move toward a high performing system and conflict and litigation risks will be managed. Your organization will not mimic dysfunctional behavior but will deliver on its promise—to do what it is intended to do.

Six weeks after the training the organization gets the report on themes, trends, and issues. You will get a clearer picture of what needs to be commended in the workplace and what needs to be corrected. This is a summary of the report that is completed during the workshop. At this stage, we can discuss your needs for further reports, such as recommendations for improvement. Remember that it is your leadership capability and skills that will enhance or handicap this process.

4. Results

4.1. Greater correlation between organizational mission and organizational achievements and clearer communication that bridges the gap between managers and workers from different generations and improved interpersonal relations in the workplace.

4.2. Enhanced problem-solving skills and less conflict and loss of team performance hours. Increase in innovative strategies.

4.3. Less resources spent on maintenance issues and more disbursements for mission challenges and imperatives; subsequently increased job satisfaction.

4.4. Reduction of passive aggressive losses, litigation threats, carelessness in the workplace and "rationalized shrinkage."

4.5. Easing-in of new employees into the work environment and limited downtime in the productivity of new hires thus money will be saved on HR staffing solutions and you will have increased productivity. The organization will thus experience a comprehensive enhanced commitment to service excellence standards.

4.6. *Fairness in staff performance appraisals across departments and sectors will lead to improved team spirit. Equitable promotions and career paths.*

4.7. *Enhancement of corporate branding and image will lead to greater customer satisfaction and CRM&M (customer relationship management and marketing). In today's world, return customers as well as referrals are essential for organizational survival.*

4.8. *Less institutional abuse and harassment litigation will also impact staff reduction and high staff turnover rates and a reduction of frequent leave of absence due to "sickism" (playing sick).*

4.9. *Less hazardous organizational environment will lead to a healthier, growth encouraging organizational culture. Organizational culture is to the organization what personality is to an individual.*

4.10. *Respect for your leadership capability and capacity and quest to define reality in diversity. The celebration of diversity will reduce destructive talk, blame and shame games, and toxicity in the system. Under your watch, the most recent diversity audit will become available.*

4.11. *Greater positive impact on nation building.*

4.12. *A legacy worth leaving behind.*

4.13. *Recognition and respect for leadership in difficult circumstances.*

4.14. *Any important strategic focus for you and your organization.*

4.15. *Knowing the difference between reality and problems.*

4.16. *Since you spend more than half your lifetime in the workplace, why not have fun?*

4.17. *Ethics in administration is often complicated by the way management treats staff and workers.*

4.18. A team commitment to professional ethics in the workplace.
4.19. A work milieu worth working in for all.

5. Program (sample)

Delivering on the organizational promise,

"EVERY STAFF MEMBER HAS AN OPPORTUNITY to Cocreate a Work Milieu Worth Working in, for All"
ORGANIZABONDING

HOST: Dr. Michael Gaffley CYC-P
DECEMBER 26-28, 2008

Day 1

1.	**9.00-9.30**	**Statement of Purpose (Casing: Apple/star)**
2.	**9.30-10.00**	**Problem Solving (Nails)**
3.	**10.00-10.15**	**Refreshments**
4.	**10.15-12.30**	**OrganizaBONDING** **OrganizaSELF** **OrganizaLEADER**
5.	**12.30-1.30**	**Lunch and Social Interactions**
6.	**1.30-2.30**	**MBTI Form G/M Self-Scoring**
7.	**2.30-4**	**TEAM Practice Applications**

NOTES:

Apple Nails
Belonging Workbook
Sit with someone you have not spent lunch with
MBTI and Funny Descriptions
Please read the evening of day one
Menu of Rewards, Motivation
Ellis Paper, Culture,
Magazines, Scissors, Glue,
Experiential Learning Models,
Essentials of Learning Organizations
Infrastructure

Day 2

1. **9.00-9.30 OrganizaTeam(SWOT)**
2. **9.30-9.45 Refreshments**
3. **9.45-10.30 OrganizaDiversity**
4. **10.30-12.00 Mobilizing Energy (Contract)**
5. **12.00-1.00 Lunch and Social Interactions**
6. **1.00-2.00 Collage Building**
7. **2.00-4.00 Applications**

Day 3

1. **9.00-9.30 Feedback**
2. **9.30-11.00 Organizarecovery**
3. **11.00-12.30 Organizaconflict**
4. **12.30-1.30 Lunch and Social Interactions**
5. **1.30-2.30 When Things Go Bump**
6. **2.30-3.30 OrganizaChange**
7. **3.30-4.30 OrganizaStrategic Scenarios**

This organizational management model has brought about a much-leaner administrative process. The model trims wasteful expenditure, reduces performance fatigue, and energizes staff. This model is particularly relevant in today's downturn of the economy. A shrinking economy impacts the organizational bottom line. When an organization is facing new challenges, it is the people in the organization that recognize the pressure. Staff members need to operate in concert in order to implement the organizational vision. When the personal stuff gets in the way of the teamwork, the organizational mission suffers.

Corporate survival during the recession resulted in organizational downsizing, with both administrative and direct labor layoffs. Staff morale often suffers as a result of organizational turbulence. The recovery phase of the recession will require strategic partnership, new employee job descriptions and new visions. Organizations need to revisit the contract between organization and staff.

A less hostile, more professional organizational culture and climate are needed in today's organizations. *Organizabonding* can both facilitate and empower supervisors to embrace and include staff on a more frequent basis in the daily decision making processes and activities. An employee can invite another employee who they do not interact with on a frequent basis to share lunch, attend a meeting or to work on a project. Professors can invite students to participate in research. Workers can invite each other to participate in committees or initiatives. Remember, that a chain is only as strong as its weakest link. Disengaged workers are potential weak links in an organization. This model is one sure way to invite commitment and to nurture engagement. *Organizabonding* will increase staff morale, decrease staff turnover and grow the staff team. Engaging in the *Organizabonding* Model will stop the guessing game. Employers will not have to view their workers with suspicion because they will know their workers. An engaged workforce spawns engaged workers.

Chapter Eight

Leadership, Leaders, and Leading

Systems thinking is a discipline for seeing wholes. It is a framework for seeing interrelationships rather than things, for seeing patterns of change rather than static "snapshots." It is a set of general principles—distilled over the course of the twentieth century, spanning fields as diverse as the physical and social sciences, engineering, and management . . . During the last thirty years, these tools have been applied to understand a wide range of corporate, urban, regional, economic, political, ecological, and even psychological systems. And system thinking is a sensibility—for the subtle interconnectedness that gives living systems their unique character.

—Peter Senge (1947-)

This brings me to leadership, a much defined and debated concept in our organizations and in our world. I want to capture my perception of leadership in a particular time frame. Peter Senge (1990) said that leadership exists when people are no longer victims of circumstances, but participate in creating new circumstances. Leadership is about creating a domain in which human beings continually deepen their understanding of reality and become more capable of participating in the unfolding of the world. Effective leadership is about satisfying the basic human needs of people in organizations. Ultimately, leadership is about inspiring and energizing the organizational missionaries or workforce and creating new realities.

Senge is on the money for me. Leadership gave me the opportunity to rework and renegotiate my life. It gave me the opportunity to become creative. The better I understood the reality of my life, my lifestyle, and my lot, the better I was able to connect with others. We often remain followers when we could be leaders because we are incapacitated by our lack of self-knowledge. And when we do become leaders, we apply leadership from our inner wellspring, our sense of self. This is particularly obvious when we hear about the stupid things that some leaders do. We have had a number of leaders who have failed their constituents, perhaps because the things they endured during childhood caused them to do the things that hurt others in their organizations. They will either add to the interpersonal conflict in the workplace or be guilty of fraud and corruption.

I believe that leaders need to always be mindful of their roots. We have to stay connected to our roots. It is the roots that gave us our sense of belonging, our identity, our opportunities to learn to trust and our safe spaces to explore life. Next, I think our cultural customs or rituals are important. During these rituals of bedtime, bath time and food time, we learn to master skills. We learn that we can make mistakes and we can try again. Our increasing competence reinforces our identity and we take up responsibility for our relationships. However, we have to identify reality. We have to learn to share tasks, roles, and responsibilities. Our capacity to share, to give generously, must be authentic, not symbolic. People will know the genuineness of our charity. They will know whether it stems from an ulterior motive or whether it is an expression of who we really are in our innermost being. The core issue is that in spite of differences in one's roots and in one's rituals, you have to be tolerant and try to understand the roots and rituals of others. You have to try and wrap your mind around why you and other people do what you do in the way that you do it.

Our home should be the first recipient of our kindness. We should not be nicer to people on the street than we are with our own flesh and blood, lest we soon sell them out in the dubious things that we do it because of the void in our primary system. We have examples of this where very popular CEOs have embellished the books of the company without even thinking about the impact of the consequences of their misdeeds on their spouse and their children. Invariably, when the heat and prosecution gets to be too much, they commit suicide, leaving their families with the shame and embarrassment. You have to find your highest calling in life, and that should always include the welfare of your wife and children, your family. Most of the current successful companies have a CEO that is also a family person. It is in fact in your family system that you learn to negotiate and nurture relationships. You learn this even if your family is dysfunctional. I believe that you cannot honor relationships in the workplace while you neglect relationships at home because the discrepancy will eventually wreak havoc on your personal life. Many people that started successful business empires have used a philosophy similar to that of Mary Kay, the cosmetic magnate: first God, then family, then business. Remember that we all have to do better and that none of us are going to get out of this life alive.

Leadership therefore means to articulate a powerful vision that can mobilize people to act to change present reality to a more realistic future for the world's children. To be a leader means to know yourself, know your limitations, know your abilities, know your strengths as well as your weaknesses. To be a leader means to know your history. To be a leader means to be the host of all the players and issues. To be a leader means to be in the middle of a bipolar tension or even multiple tensions. To be a leader means to have strength to be tolerant. To be a leader means not to give up on the human relationships in the workplace. We know the effect on children when a child in custodial care has ten teachers or twelve social workers in one year. To be the leader means to work at your issues, your relationships and your organizational mission. As you work, you do not just make manifest your work ethic, but you are also modeling your philosophy of life and the value you attach to people, your best organizational asset. If you are the leader, you do not allow yourself to get bogged down with complexities; you lead the change process by caring for self and nurturing your staff. To be the leader means to be in continuous discomfort. To be the leader means to wrestle and not rest but to find ways of bringing resolution in the face of conflict or challenge. When I investigated quality in human services, quality in this sense means being fit for purpose; I found that leadership was the key to designing and delivering the organizational promise. Leaders who do not know the regulations governing their business, leaders who cannot engage people, and leaders who cannot measure and manage the money constitute a hazard in their organizational system. Leaders who are not naïve but are players in the political system are prepared to get the best returns for their organization. Many leaders have knowledge but lack wisdom, and this weakens them. A metaphor from the life of a great scientist will illustrate this point. The scientist was doing a series of lectures around the country. One day he said to his chauffeur that he was getting tired and that he was going to cancel the lecture for the next evening at a small town university. His chauffeur begged him not but to rather allow the chauffeur to do the lecture instead. He assured the scientist that he knew the lecture so well because he has been in his company for a long time. Well, the chauffeur pretended to be the scientist and the scientist donned the chauffeur's uniform and then the scientist took a seat in the back of the auditorium. The chauffeur presented the lecture as the scientist. The lecture went so well that there was enough time for questions from the august audience. Right in front was an eminent scholar who raised his hand and asked a very complex question. The scientist responded to the question by saying that the man was asking so basic a question that even his chauffeur at the back of the room would be able to answer. The chauffeur had the wisdom but the scientist had the knowledge. In a similar vein, Albert Einstein reminded us that imagination is more important than knowledge. He said that knowledge will get you from point A to point B and that imagination will get you anywhere. Imagination is the threshold to creativity and is the only condition for hope to survive and thrive. For me, imagination was the nemesis of my present reality. Dead people give neither problems nor challenges in the workplace because they imagine no more.

May I remind you that my challenge here is to educate, inform and to agitate with permission and that if I succeed in irritating you then you have the invitation to the elevation of your mind-set? Leaders need to remain teachable. Leaders need to let go of the need to let popularity massage their egos. I suggest that my reputation is what you know about me, but my integrity is what I know about myself. It is with my integrity that I fall asleep peacefully every evening.

Today, organizations operate in a post-industrial, post-modern, post-literate, post-Christian, cocreative, knowledge—and information-driven, entertainment-craving milieu. Many age-old traditions suffer as a result of the generation gap. We have to rethink work, our way of working and ourselves as workers. Research findings and ever-emerging new paradigms are forcing us to rethink work. We are not doing the best we can. And if we do not, we are failing our constituents and stakeholders. Leadership is most effective when it leads to social transformation. I could take you back to the gate through which I entered the leadership forum. I could tell you about my involvement with youth leadership development, diversity training, transformations and transitions, typologies, and ideologies in my native country. However, I would much rather focus on my most recent experiential learning experience and personal transformation. I have worked with young people who were sexually, physically, and/or emotionally abused.

Their families rejected them and the abused young people were often blamed for the dysfunction and struggles of the family. I could often mirror my own rejection and anger in their anger and rejection, but this only succeeded in maintaining the status quo. I had to learn to transcend the awful things in my past in the creative things I was doing in the present, thus creating stepping stones to my future. These stepping stones were in fact part of the solid foundation that I was reconstructing for my life. I thus helped myself and others to do something that will make our past mishaps and misfortunes belong to our history and not to our future.

My children and I have taken to wave runners. In this process I have rediscovered some valuable leadership lessons. These lessons are underpinned in a process based on and enhanced by constant communication.

Vignette Number 1

To the same degree that you accelerate, you have power to control the steering mechanism. You cannot steer or control direction at idle speed. You have to open the throttle and unleash energy. Your steering/directing is emission-dependent. It is the "exhaust" that controls the steering and that optimizes maneuverability of the craft. In leadership terminology, that would imply that unless leadership is progressive, in the reality of the moment, it will lose its ability to influence the way to go and get others on board, sharing the vision, mission, and commitment. Our "emission" as leaders produces consequences. What we "emit" as leaders through verbal or nonverbal communication, role modeling, or the ability to inspire, can be legendary or real, authentic, or symbolic. Sometimes, omissions and commissions may have the same effect in engaging followers, but for different reasons or motivational forces. What power, control and influence issues and themes have emerged from your metaphors? Outcomes may look the same, but what was the intent?

Vignette Number 2

The person at the rear has a greater impact on maneuverability and direction. In leadership, we often ensure that we have the people that support us on board when in fact the ones that are left behind can so easily sabotage the vision and mission. If people don't get what they want, they take it anyway. An example will illustrate this point. If a worker comes to the boss and asks for time off in order to attend to a sick child, the boss may refuse such permission and remind the worker that he or she has schedules or reports that are due by the end of the business day. Well, the worker will stay but will call in sick the next day or come to work late for a couple of days. The worker may feel why he or she should care for the company if the company does not care about him or her or their family. They will then proceed in this mind-set to make copies of articles from magazines for their personal use; they will make copies for their children's school projects and make copies for their Sunday school lessons in the boss's time. In 1985 United Airlines filed for Chapter 11 bankruptcy. They came out of this by offering workers profit sharing and other benefits in lieu of a pay raise. In 2002 United Airlines again filed for bankruptcy protection. This time they stated that it was difficult to negotiate with the unions because the workers feel that they still have not received the pay raise they wanted. The workers were feeling that they owed the company no loyalty because the company had not been loyal to the workers. These kinds of actions may often damage the enterprise or organization. Leadership is the skilful apportionment of vision commensurate with ability. Why do we often insist on the continuation of strategies that do not work?

Vignette Number 3

The veil of our arrogance dims the radiance of our personality. There I was fifty years young, good parent, teacher—alas, not good at wave running. Very soon, my otherwise radiant personality was dimmed by the present reality out on the ocean. Currently so many people are hurt in the corporate and human services world because of the ineptitude and lack of integrity of people in leadership. Reality affirms that they have confused reputation with integrity. Reputation is what others think about us and integrity is what I know about myself. The personality domain continues to be a focal point in debates about leadership.

As both an academic and practitioner of leadership, I encourage learners to have a solid grounding in the leadership literature. This literature has been written by both university faculty and by leadership practitioners in the field. By reading these materials, I hope that the information that you glean will inform your own practice of leadership. In addition to reading and being knowledgeable about leadership, I also encourage you to practice your leadership skills. The acquisition of both knowledge and skills are central to your leadership roles in your workplace and your community.

Let me say something about change. The jury is still out on whether it is the followers who are most ready for change or whether leaders are ready for change. I have seen evidence of both. I have seen leaders who are passionately leading change, struggling to get followers on board. My advice is to sell them the law of the harvest. Show them the bounty that will ensue for all. Give them the roadmap, for your vision with both rules for the road and a demarcation of how to reach the destination. Likewise, I have seen organizations where the organization is ready to move but they are struggling to get the leader on board. This is especially true in smaller organizations. It is difficult to change these organizations. Sometimes the only option is for you to leave the organization. Even a sequential synopsis or brief summary and timeline about change in any life or organization will reveal that change does not happen in sequence along a straight line. Confronting change is like a perpetual roller-coaster ride: once started, it gains momentum in spite of disconnects, lateral movements, and cerebral musings about how to stop it. The players may all be at different levels of perception, each one looking at the tapestry of change. Some just see the downside of change as if they were looking at the back of the tapestry while others may become intolerant because they are beginning to see the shape on the right side. The change process can be frustrating because you make progress and then you experience setbacks, it seems that everyone is on board and then you identify some opposition to the change efforts.

The golden rule is that everyone must remain teachable. Authentic change in organizations is dependent on authentic change in the leaders. In order for change to be sustainable, you have to work together. We are best when we function as a team. To be a team means to engage with others. Be sure to acknowledge that there are different positions and functions on a team; although different and distinguishable once you separate them, you no longer have a team. You may be in different departments and/or locations, but you need to be firmly committed to the organizational mission and purpose. Do not allow anyone to sabotage the organizational vision and goal because it just saps the organizational energy. Organizations that spend more money on maintenance of human relations, interpersonal conflict and fear of litigation costs are wasting valuable resources that should have funded the organizational mission. At all costs, do not allow personality clashes to dominate the organizational culture because if you leave these differences unchecked you will soon have spiraling conflict to contend with. My maxim here is that unobtrusive intervention is preferred to direct confrontation.

Paradigms are changing and it means that mind-sets have to change. Change is a perfect opportunity to give voice and stature to everyone in the organization. For too long we have drowned the voice of the masses in our organization. Change is both crucible and wellspring. The better way to be creative is to transcend our past in what and how we do business now.

The choice is to be pallbearer of the past or flame bearer of the future.

Leadership is of paramount importance in the multifaceted human services field in which our work with children, youth, and families is firmly embedded. On the one hand, we are aware of the need for leaders with the capability and capacity to lead, and on the other, for leaders who can facilitate capability and capacity building in the next generation of leaders. What advice will we give our leaders?

We are indeed shaped by our past and are always challenged to transcend our past in order to be effective, contemporary leaders. It should be our goal to build the leadership capability and capacity in civic agencies and institutions that can meet the current challenges as well as future needs of an ever-changing society. Leaders, we need to make the world a better place for our children and young people. This is a leadership lesson we have to fast-track in the post-apartheid South Africa. However, leaders will not be able to make a qualitative difference to effect the change that will meet the needs of a more diverse population, changing economy and technology of the twenty-first century unless they are a product of the personal change crucible. Leadership is interactive-dependent and implies a paradoxical integration of being and doing, and leaders who do this well will make a meaningful difference to the quality of life of others and themselves. Current leadership research informs us of CEOs who talk about their resistance to change. We need leaders in human services agencies who do not bury their heads and dig in their heels for the wrong reasons.

It is savvy for organizations to have their primary focus on outcomes and results, the bottom line. This is a bad omen especially for not-for-profit and volunteer organizations. In child and youth care for example, the bottom line is a constant bi-polar creative tension of human dignity in tandem with the focus on the future, the horizon and its concomitant possibilities that can promote positive youth development. In child and youth care, our bottom line is a constant bi-polar creative tension of human dignity in tandem with the focus on the future, the horizon and its concomitant possibilities. We dare not discard any client because of present "unacceptable" circumstances. Circumstances can change and the client has the power to change, over time.

It is said that psychiatrists often mimic the behavior of their clients. I see this happening in the human services field where the professional conduct of leaders is sometimes dubious. Leaders are oftentimes more dysfunctional than the clients. You need only observe the idiosyncratic behavioral styles at any regional or international assemblage of our field. Just observe the culturally inappropriate and insensitive innuendo and disrespect. To bring it closer to home, just reflect on the reluctance to deal with destructive "lounge talk" that happens in many agencies or observe the "groupie culture" at conferences. Here is the challenge: we can stay as we are or we can run away, but we cannot hide. Sometimes in concealing we are actually revealing our authentic self. Our lack of leadership capability and capacity will be conspicuous by its absence. Let us then look at the leadership challenge.

Be Visionary Risk-Takers

Vision is the first critical dimension of effective leadership. Without vision, there is little or no sense of purpose or direction in any organization. The direction gives the organization an identity. Without this identity, efforts drift aimlessly as people struggle for meaning. The lack of purpose leads to a lack of coordination among the work units in an organization and divisive infighting among staff. The articulation of your vision energizes and mobilizes the leadership process and gives your followers a map of your expectations as well as the rules for the road. Vision always brings the future into focus, it motivates involvement, it implies hope, and instils courage. The wisdom literature in the Bible states that "where there is no vision the people perish." Vision is one of the paramount observable characteristics of effective leadership. Clearly articulated vision, purpose, and core values are best created from the mind-set of aspiration rather than desperation. The vision may be general or specific, but it is the leader's passion and the mental image of a better condition than what currently exists. The primary challenge for human services agency leadership is discussed in Senge (1990) who said, "When people truly share a vision they are connected, bound together by a common aspiration" (p. 206). President Nelson Mandela made a public statement in the courthouse during his trial for sabotage and treason in 1964. He said, "I have cherished the ideal of a democratic and free society in which all persons live together in harmony and with equal opportunities. It is an ideal which I hope to live for and achieve. But if need be, it is an ideal for which I am prepared to die." In 1994, after being imprisoned for twenty-seven years, after much bloodshed, pain, tears, and the death of people in the liberation struggle, Mandela became the first black democratically elected president of South Africa. His vision attracted people to his movement even when the movement was banned and had to operate "underground" in pursuit of its goal and passion.

Human services agencies need leaders who will enable staff, children, youth, families, and the community to build a vision for the agency—to articulate a vision and be able to make that vision concrete to others. Leaders need to provide an environment and culture in the organization in which creativity, risk-taking, and experimentation in pursuit of excellence are shared by all partners; and to understand, facilitate, and manage change in themselves, others, and in their organizations.

Supervision and Delegation

The leader cannot do everything, alone. You need to delegate tasks, roles and responsibilities to people, your staff, your team. On the one end of the continuum you do not want to be too involved in the execution of assignments and on the other you do not want to be too detached. However you want to remain committed to quality. I was very curious to know why the turnover of staff was highest in the lower paid staff like custodial workers of the residential facility that I was directing at the time. Upon investigation I found that this staff component was almost always hired in crisis mode. They were told how to clean the cottages and were assigned to their tasks. No sooner had they started their employment when they were fired. This situation repeated itself so many times. Then I had a brilliant idea and that was to clean the cottage and to have it in ship shape at the time that we interviewed the next applicants. We conducted the interviews in the cottages that needed custodial staff. We showed them what it looked like and asked them whether they could keep it that way. Surprisingly, that was the end of the high staff turnover of custodial workers. Leaders need to not only describe successful outcomes but should at best be able to show models of excellence.

Embrace Diversity

Our agencies are becoming more diverse and navigating a changing workplace is both art and science. The "people factor" is critical in human services. However, cultural chauvinism will not promote teamwork in the twenty-first-century workplace, which relies on internationalization and globalization. Harry Triandis (1993), the godfather of cross-cultural psychology, observed that culture's influence on organizational behavior is that it operates at such a deep level that people are not aware of its influences. It results in unexamined patterns of thought that seem so natural that most theorists of social behavior fail to take them into account. Many aspects of organizational theories produced in one culture may be inadequate in other cultures. Leaders will model respect, understanding, and appreciation for all people; respond to the needs of persons with special needs and to the needs of a multicultural and economically diverse society; and function effectively in a multilingual community. Embracing the diversity mosaic does not necessarily imply that you either embrace the "cookie-cutter" approach or the "melting pot" approach. However, perceptual prejudice, stereotyping, xenophobia, victimarchy (a word coined by Warren Farrell in *The Myth of Male Power* to describe a society that conceives of its members as victims perpetually unable to direct their own affairs or to control their own destinies), or any other trend, fad, or wave can lead to the onset of leadership scotoma. Scotoma is a blind spot or lack of vision in a part or area of the visual field. People from diverse backgrounds can make an effective community without having to display an attitude of superiority. Diversity is a reality and cultural mismatches are symptomatic of systemic failure. Current and emerging leaders in the human services sector will be adept at capability and capacity building, cultural competency and ethical conduct. The call to effective leadership implies an obligation to maximize those opportunities for all children, youth, and families from diverse cultural backgrounds to become functional in spite of the odds.

Have Excellent, Professional, and Ethical Human Relation Skills

It costs nothing to have good, decent, professional, workplace conduct and manners. Leaders will respond to the needs of other staff members, children, students, parents, and community; facilitate communication that yields teamwork, consensus, and inquiry; and help resolve conflicts and manage stress. The behavior of followers is often validated by the leadership example. Parenting has taught us that behavior is context-dependent. The quality of interaction between people higher up in the organizational hierarchy is replicated by those in the lower part of the hierarchy. Professional conduct, etiquette and simple human courtesies are certainly embodied in good practice and are a sure way of optimizing leadership effectiveness and success.

Know the Work of Their Agencies

The work of leaders in the corporate world is pretty clear cut because they pay market-related salaries commensurate with work experience, they focus on their product, and the bounty displayed on the bottom line is evidence of excellent leadership. However, leaders of human services agencies, school districts, and other organizational structures or institutions will work with others to facilitate the creation of a safe and healthy environment where the growth of young people, both academic and social, takes place. They will promote learning for customers, staff, parents, and other community members; have knowledge of their organization, structure, function, and purpose in a democratic society; understand stages of human development; have an understanding of the care continuum; have knowledge of strengths-based assessment and evaluation; and know how to assess and evaluate staff and program effectiveness and to promote excellence in both. Finally, they will collaborate with other social service agencies, other state agencies, and business and industry.

Organizational Culture is the Key to Success

Culture is to the organization what personality is to the individual. Agencies are expected to design developmental plans and identify developmental goals for clients. Agencies are embarking on training programs for their staff. However, nothing is being done to develop the organizations in which staff has to perform their functions. The wellness of agencies as change agents is often questionable. Our often-hostile staff relations and toxic environment is not therapeutic.

A tantalizing thought often haunted me. From whose perspective are we viewing best practice? If you tell the story of the three little pigs from the wolf's perspective, you will no doubt have a different ending. Be aware of the many points of view variance. Likewise if cultural mismatch was the pinnacle perspective, conduct disorder would not be the assessment. Policymakers, politicians and funders often have no idea of the real struggle with clients in a cottage during transitions, meal times or in any twenty-four-hour period.

Model Leadership

Human service agency leaders will be intellectually stimulated and reflective. They will keep abreast of new technological advances and innovative ideas by reading magazines, professional journals and by visiting appropriate websites. They have to be lifelong learners. Leaders have to take their professional development seriously as well as take responsibility for the mentoring of the next generation of leaders. They will have a sense of humor and self knowledge and high self-esteem; be ethical and accept responsibility for their own actions and behaviors; function as generalists who make connections between different fields; have a clear sense of power and authority; identify, create, and use resources; understand and utilize short—and long-range planning processes. They need to live a well balance life because they do not have the luxury of attending to one pressing need at a time. They will exhibit skills in marketing and public relations; and have an astute understanding of the politics in their agency, system, and community.

Empowerment

Leadership is about opportunity and action. When an opportunity arises and it is not met with appropriate action, nothing changes. Change and making a difference is at the heart of the nexus of opportunity and action. If people are not able to seize the moment, an opportunity to lead will be wasted. People need both capability and capacity to take required action. Taking risks is an important component of gaining mastery over one's personal and professional life. The biggest risk for leaders is empowerment. Leaders must allocate the resources and decision-making authority to their followers and give them the freedom to fail without fear of retribution. Zero tolerance does not lead to empowerment. Warren Bennis (1994) described empowerment as the power reciprocal requiring transformative leadership in the individual as well as the organization. This transformation requires a keen sense of judgment and the wise and judicious use of power by the leader.

Leaders must also know what is right and what is necessary. This has to do partially with the ultimate nature and quality of the innate character and personality of the leader that enables them to make fair decisions. In this sense, the faith and loyalty of followers is not lost even in the most difficult human encounters. Truth and honesty are at the heart of judgment. Leaders must be willing to investigate the facts; often, it is just when they have the least amount of time to do so. Human services agency leaders have to know that facts are interpreted truths. It is never the facts of the matter but the facts *for* the matter. We know that behavior is purposive. Whether it is the reporter or the reported, know that facts do not speak for themselves.

Empowerment implies knowledge and nurturance of the most important attributes of leader effectiveness: (a) personal knowledge, (b) knowledge based on content, (c) problem-solving ability, (d) ability to critically analyze and develop visions for the future, (e) effective communication skills, (f) ability to translate visions into goals, (g) risk-taking ability, (h) good sense of judgment, (i) flexibility, and (j) willingness to work within an organization as a team member. The difficulty in defining leadership and extricating the most important attributes lies in the uniqueness of each individual leader. Every leader brings something original to the workplace. You cannot produce a leader from a recipe, formula, model, or mold.

We know that the work of particular leaders differs greatly because of differences in individual characteristics, situational variables, and organizational contexts. The work and protocols of the principal firefighter is different yet, in many instances, the same as that of the senior pastor of a church or the principal of a school. The situation is further complicated when the concepts of management and leadership are applied to human services agencies. These organizations often are ambiguous; frequently, they have no profit motive and the bottom line is absent. The lack of focus on the money that they can or should be making, often make them look like they are in business without a specific purpose. They also seem to want to help everybody to the degree that they run out of resources and they are eventually closed down because they make their own programs vulnerable because of this "soft commitment" to help in spite of the realism that they cannot help everybody. So we, largely drawn from the social science, educational, and youth serving community, are people generally employed in nonprofit organizations. We like to define leadership as the ability of an individual to influence the values, attitudes, beliefs, and actions of others by working with and through them in relationships in order to restore their functionality and to optimize the organization's mission and purpose. Management is usually defined as the ability to integrate the different organizational functions such as policies, procedures, systems, and equipment—for the purpose of organizing the component necessary to accomplish the mission and purpose. Managers handle the day to day complexities of the business. The role of leadership for learning organizations is described by Senge (1990) in this way:

> Leaders are designers, stewards, and teachers. They are responsible for building organizations where people continually expand their capabilities to understand complexity, clarify vision, and improve shared mental modes . . . they are responsible for learning (p.340).

Proceed with Vigilance

Our technologically advanced world is witnessing its own inability to stem the current shedding of blood caused by waves of terrorist attacks. Vigilance is a village effort. One person on his or her own cannot make America, South Africa or any country, safe. Leadership is the vehicle through which change will be effected. The trajectory of world events is evidence of a leadership crisis. The concomitant miasma created by those leaders who have failed not so much because of poor business sense, but rather ethical failure, challenges us to rethink leadership. Leadership is the ideal tool to transform and liberate us and our organizations from being prisoners of the past to becoming pioneers of the future. Leadership can take us from trouble to triumph and from fear to faith. In spite of the continuing debate about charismatic and values-based leadership, we should continue to explore the effect of personal faith as a leadership attribute. I have been in contact with many leaders and one distinctive feature that keep them anchored in the face of diverse and complex challenges and setbacks, is their personal faith. By faith I am not referring to a specific denominational or religious faith but faith in a higher power. I have come across this faith in leaders who were adherents of Christian, Jewish, Islamic, and Hindu faith traditions.

The Leadership Manhattan

We will utilize the New York City skyline as a graphic for the following concerns. Human services agency leaders will deal with a provocative phenomenon that plays out in the daily lives of those people who might be in the wrong position in an organization or the system, and who continue to live unfulfilled lives. The delusion of indulgence has made them indifferent, experts of the art of masking, hiding, and, pretence. Holding on to a position for the wrong reason constitutes a risk for self and others. Continuing conflict in the workplace poses a challenge to leaders. More and more employees are taking legal action because of employment discrimination, affirmative action, sexual harassment, violence, and bullying practices in the workplace. Managers spend at least one third of the company's time in dealing with conflict. Staff conflict in the therapeutic milieu is a key toxin in the onset of organizational dysfunction.

Workplace compassion has been catapulted as a prominent issue since the events of 9/11. A compassionate response is indicative of the quality of both leadership and workplace. How does the workplace respond to disaster and to grief? Does the workplace mourn the loss of a loved one with the worker who is grieving this loss? Ethics and ethical dilemmas in the workplace demand our attention. Professional gossip and destructive lounge talk during tea breaks are a growing menace in the workplace. Ethical leadership will be essential in our work with human beings who cannot afford another disaster in their lives. Current events involving questionable ethical behavior of many business and church leaders remind us that the responsibility for an ethical organization belongs to its most senior leaders first. It is becoming more and more obvious that business decisions are no longer made because it is the right thing to do. Business decisions are made because they are affordable. Cutting corners and even turning a blind eye to an injustice or what is tantamount to cheating on the job has become operative words in the workplace decision-making processes. We are learning more of construction companies who, in the process of trying to save money are in fact compromising the safety of others by skimping on quality and specifications. Cranes, bridges, and buildings are collapsing and inferior products that constitute a hazard to occupants of buildings are imported from China. Just think about the inferior dry walls in many housing developments that have to be replaced.

Leadership Context

Leadership takes place in a context. It emerges from within us as we engage communities, civic, and professional life. Since it takes place in context, it is important to first consider the changes taking place around us—changes that are literally transforming the world as we experience it. Wealth distribution has a profound impact on the social landscape. What is the product of unemployment, poor skills, low income, poor housing, high-risk crime environments, ill health, and fractured families—social exclusion? To be socially excluded means to be disengaged, disconnected, detached, and this detachment has many ramifications for leaders and policymakers. This large percentage of people is often powerless and voiceless until they grab the world's attention as a result of one or other calamity. This social exclusion happens to the poor not by choice but by design. It is often government that lumps people together in projects, townships and neighborhoods. The poor is often used by power hungry despots as bargaining chips in their war with the government. The poor is used as soldiers in suicide bombings and as both weapons and shields in terror attacks. The poor is often the casualty in regime change and the overthrow of governments. The U.S. president George W. Bush in his commencement address to the United States Coast Guard Academy in May 2003 stated that more than half the world's population—nearly three billion people—are forced to survive on less than two dollars per day. Billions of men and women can scarcely imagine the benefits of modern life because they have never experienced them. The danger is that if they have nothing, they have nothing to lose. It is no wonder that cartels and drugs are gaining ground. The drug trade is flourishing and often swells the state coffers in spite of the irreparable damage caused, especially to children and families.

Poverty is not a shame, it is just very inconvenient. For the poor, poverty is not a matter of definition. It is the harsh reality that poverty has a paralyzing effect on individuals and it shapes societies. Verbal categorizing and stereotyping does not dissipate poverty. Defining a poverty line, judging the behavior of the poor, and tracing the causes of poverty are good but not good enough. Leaders should not assume that the poor have no pride and power. It is indeed tough for children, youth, and families to overcome the heavy odds of poverty, ignorance, and scarce resources. Government on its own is not going to eradicate poverty. The eradication of poverty will be a public-private partnership. Every leader in every organization should embrace as one of the organizational goals, the eradication of poverty.

Authentic Leadership

You are hopefully aware of the current mood that is sweeping the global village. People, and more especially young people, seem to be cynical and frustrated at this time when the government continues to warn about the possibility of more terrorist attacks and is not able to guarantee homeland safety and security. People seem to have lost their optimistic flair and replaced it with one of pessimism, despair, and disillusionment, globally.

The study of leadership has never been as vital and needed as now when there is a renewed search for meaning to life. Viktor Frankl (1988) posited that the striving to find a meaning in one's life is the primary motivational force in man.

One can distinguish symbolic involvement from authentic engagement in this field. What is authentic leadership? The sheer number of theorists who have tried to define leadership, is indicative of the impossibility of reducing a complex process to a simple statement. Jim Kouzes and Barry Posner (2002) define leadership as the art of mobilizing others to want to struggle for shared aspirations.

Trying to define leadership is like defining the shape of a human nose. Noses might be classified into shapes and sizes. However, everyone's nose is different. Everyone has a nose, but everyone's nose is different. Likewise everyone's leadership style will be different yet similar. Leaders, according to the theorists, must recognize, own, and be comfortable with their unique leadership style, viewing it as a positive style. Such recognition emerges, nurtured by ongoing self-reflection. Personal knowledge of strengths and the capacity to compensate for weaknesses are first steps in achieving positive self-regard (Bennis and Goldsmith 1997). Self-reflection enables one to arrive at critical choice points. Within each developmental stage there are tasks to be accomplished that enable a person to move into the next stage. Being able to accept and healthily use criticism through self-reflection is an achievement, yet it is not without feelings of emotional discomfort and restlessness. There are legitimate choices to be made. Leaders, the theory goes, must strive to gain more and more personal knowledge, as we learn from Senge (1990). He called this a personal mastery, yet personal knowledge is only one kind of knowledge needed to produce effective leadership.

In any professional field, knowledge establishes credibility—a critical component of leadership. A knowledge base is not something to have and keep; it must be periodically renewed. It demands that one remain current, and one way of remaining current is to review the literature on a periodic basis. Remaining current is, as one businessman described it, a goal without a finish line.

Leadership requires a critical analysis of process and strategy. Leaders engage in complex mental tasks. They are alert to contextual evolving patterns. The uniqueness of leaders is that they dream, of course, but that they also have the capability and capacity to manage the achievement of those dreams. In this sense, a leader must begin with the goal, and then do everything in order to reach it. It's a matter of planning backward, beginning with the goal. The urgency of effective and honest communication cannot be overstated. This, in itself, will bond diverse and independent people into a single enterprise. This kind of communication includes more than just clarity. There must be a genuine open door policy, a genuinely approachable attitude. An effective leader must have "conquered his own ego problems" and be able to listen to criticisms. "Unfortunately, much more common are leaders who have a sense of purpose and genuine vision but little ability to foster systemic understanding" (Senge 1990). That is the essence of the "learning organization." The mastery of communication is inseparable from effective leadership (Bennis 1994). Leaders must be able to speak, write, and listen in order to gain support and cooperation from followers.

Teaching Change

The undertaking of change will be a difficult one as Warren Belasco (1990) demonstrates in *Appetite for Change* as he weaved a metaphor about teaching an elephant to dance. He emphasized how organizations are tied to the past by tradition or success. Like powerful elephants, they are bound by memory of earlier constraints, which may no longer be in existence. This pessimism also extends into human services agency leadership where a number of traditional constraints and concepts must be understood and challenged in order for the "good news" to become a reality. For systems thinking to be effectively implemented in the child and youth care system, requires the individual care giver, or social worker, psychologist, teacher, and administrator to all see themselves as a part of a larger entity. Role players would begin to focus on interdependence and interaction rather than on a simple cause and effect relationship. Senge (1990) stated that "systems thinking" is a discipline for seeing wholes. It is a framework for seeing interrelationships rather than things, for seeing patterns of change rather than "snapshots." We therefore need to remind ourselves about the purpose of the human services field. It is not a breeding ground for political opportunism and social control. It seeks to enhance the science of healing and wholeness and to perfect the art of caring. Just rearranging individual prejudices is not change. Sometimes the systems have to change because is not a humane and safe place for children. In human services agencies, the maxim remains, first do no harm, (then) promote functionality. This is often not easy. Leadership is thus for tough people because often the prevailing system will do everything to maintain the status quo. In this system, the challenges are often subtle, implied, or the result of some innuendo or political agenda. Leading change is the best way of teaching change. Sometimes leaders can become overwhelmed by peripety and a reversal of fortunes for the organization. However, in spite of sudden changes in the internal and external organizational environment, leaders can lead change instead of becoming mired in complexity and the status quo. In leading change I want to paint a few brush strokes on the canvas of change.

Motivation and Measurement: What motivates someone to do something that he or she has to do, but, does not want to do? You may think of children who know that they have to do their homework, but choose not to do it. They know and will face the consequences of their errancy, time after time, after time. Equally valid is the addict who is admitted to a treatment center but does not adhere to the prescribed treatment plan. *What motivates is only starting the engines.* You have to engage the transmission (change) to get movement. Movement is measurable. Measuring is the Siamese twin of managing. If you cannot measure it you cannot manage it. If you cannot manage it you cannot measure it.

Articulation and Action: Can you articulate meaning? Is it expedient? Does it compromise any of the stakeholders? Self-knowledge, knowledge based on content, problem-solving ability, ability to critically analyze and develop visions for the future, effective communication skills, ability to translate visions into goals, risk-taking ability, good sense of judgment, flexibility, and willingness to work within an organization as a team member are the actual and potential competencies of leadership. Your job is to enable and to facilitate the "becoming" of others. The starting block however is an inventory of *current ability* as well as where they are at, momentarily in their mindset. Be cautious with assumptions. This will set the stage for an attitude alignment in order to co-create meaning. As head of the treatment planning team, I had to often bite my tongue and remind myself that the power to change is with the client and family.

Politics and Process: This is a marathon race not a sprint event. It is a process. Something can be most beautiful on paper but when you authentically engage the shoes come off and the odor can be toxic. Need I say more? My friends there are those who imagine that you can leave the politics out. Your political naivety does not negate the political savvy of even an opportunist. What a grave error. Politics is at play all the time whether expressed in micro-inequality or innuendo or manifest behavior. You have to be a player adept at playing the political games people play. People love power games, mind games and to be in control.

Values and Virtues: Decisions, choices and actions are pre-conditioned and are influence-dependent. Disregarding values do not make them disappear. Without virtue your best efforts are flawed. Talking about values, remember that your reputation is what others think about you. However, you have to sleep with your integrity as your company. Your reputation does not join you on your pillow. If that was so more people would suffer from sleep deprivation because they would be too excited to fall asleep.

Ideas and Information: You values are best seen in the expression of your ideas. Everyone's ideas have value. Ideas, like icebergs, often have concealed thoughts behind them. The good thing about ideas and life is that, that which one wants to hide most, is most obvious. Ideas convey information.

Culture and Circumstances: Circumstances are NOT the sum total of culture. Like the ocean is to fish, culture is to human beings. As children, we started to navigate the sea of life enveloped in the safety of our family and culture. Culture colors everything. Nothing happens in a vacuum. It is indeed wise to understand the culture and not to judge the circumstance from where you stand.

Timing and Tuning: Perception is a critical reality. "Strike on the spot while the iron is hot" is good advice. We often miss those golden opportunities to accelerate the change process when we do not respond in time and in tune with the moment. Show compassion in the moment of need and not later when it is comfortable for you to show compassion.

Obligation and Opportunity: You have chosen to accept responsibility for changing the status quo for all, occupational hazards and all. Don't quit when the going gets tough. Commitment and cost are tandem partners in empowering others. Your knowledge base is an asset to be utilized.

Resistance and Relationship: The bounce of the ball is a good barometer of the interpersonal and intrapersonal. One can only bounce the ball to another if you have the ball. Human beings are just that, human beings. We do not always have to analyze why the ball was not bounced to us. Just keep on bouncing the ball to others and soon they and you will enjoy the interaction. A paradoxical integration between being and doing exists. Be prepared. Do not personalize. Respond to challenges and encourage collaboration. Relationship is key in the management of change. Nurture and maintain healthy, growth producing, professional relationships in and around the organizational context.

Yen (desire) **and Yields:** People have a strong desire for meaning. Often the known has more meaning than the unknown. Trust is a needed cornerstone in our engagement. Harness energy by highlighting the possible harvest. Emphasizing the returns, dividends, or yield can motivate. WIIFM is often everybody's bottom line. However, the new has to be born through the dying of the old.

The Transitional Period

During the period of transition, the letting go of the old, and almost in tandem activity of embracing the new, leaders have to be aware of the impact that this phase in the human services agency's cycle of change has on both the leader and the followers. Sustained primary or first—order change is difficult in any structured organization. However, leaders are not always prepared for, or cognizant of, the forces and factors inherent in the transformational change. This is the time when most people feel that they are in a dessert or dry place. They are like a voice crying in the dessert, in a worst-case scenario, simply feeling deserted. Leaders have to be cognizant of both mental and emotional states of followers and take appropriate action in the transition period. Often the energy spent in damage control renders the leader defunct to nip in the bud, attempts to sabotage the vision.

A child who was admiring a shiny new car parked in the street outside an old house, asked a man who appeared from the house whose car it was. "Mine," the man said. "Mister, this shiny new car and that old house do not match." "Oh, my brother gave it to me as a birthday present." "Gee, mister, I wish . . ."

What do you think he wished for? I suppose many of us would wish for a brother like that! He said, "Gee, mister, I wish I was a brother like that." I suppose that it is easier to want instead of wanting to be the brother. We have to be the leader we want.

Development of a Pinnacle Perspective

Development of a pinnacle perspective will enhance your systems thinking skills. The client is human and has feelings just like you. Get to the point where the real things really matter. Get to the point where you are not as obsessive-compulsive about everything. Learn that your way is not the only right way. Learn to know that the most important thing to know is to know what we do not know. Learning can only take place when you admit that you do not know. I realize that there is so much about life that I do not know.

The personal twenty-first-century leadership quest is a call to grapple with current issues and at the same time to let go of conclusions based on past experience and centuries of pain. We are both the continuation of previous generations and a unique expression of that continuity. Many leaders are identifiable by the baggage and unfinished business of previous encounters that reduced their speech to oral poison. They are both paradoxically anchored in and driven by past conditioning forces and dispensations. As much as they want to be heralds of their leadership vision, they often falter and give credence to self-fulfilling prophecy. Many potential leaders remain just that because they either lack the will to overcome the odds or to accept the challenge. The irony is that whether they step up to the leadership plate or not, the masses will continue to be led, the ball can continue to bounce irrespective of who participates. The issue in leadership is that we participate not because of but in spite of.

My late father used to say, "Young man, get enough education so that you will never have to look up to anyone and then get a little bit more so that you do not look down on anyone." It is your turn at bat. Celebrate joy, enjoy, and let your joy overflow and envelop your contemporaries, even your adversaries. We are more productive when we are having fun. Praise improves the performance of people. You can force your way through a crowd but not into one person's heart and leaders who are wrapped up in themselves, contribute little, make very small packages, and are like dynamite without a spark/fuse.

Leadership is about capability and capacity building. Leadership is allowing and energizing self and others to become functional, cocreatively. Thus, be aware that if people do not get what they want, they take it anyway, anyhow. Ignore a baby's attachment cries, and observe the dysfunction during adolescence. Be the leader you would want others to be. Long live the noble work we do in human services agencies. Leadership is about hosting others by inviting them to bring their contribution to the finding of solutions, visions and policies that can make a qualitative difference to people, to our environment, and to our finite world.

Every individual is born with innate abilities, gifts, and talents. These constitutional elements have to be honed to match the skills needed in the workplace. Honing these skills is what I refer to as capability and capacity building. You have to assist workers to reach deep inside themselves in order to connect with their real abilities and skills. Sometimes just helping them with their self-esteem builds their capability and capacity, and optimizes their skill sets. Sometimes they may not have good communication skills or writing skills. These skills can all be sharpened through remedial steps or a supportive relationship.

At this time the world is beckoning for a leader that can inspire. We need leaders with integrity, and credibility because leadership is about change, progress, and effectiveness. I would much rather follow a leader that inspires than one whose idle words and rhetoric is just showmanship. That leader will be great as an actor but his or her acts will not get followers and there will be no flowers or harvest.

Chapter Nine

Diversity

A community is like a ship; everyone ought to be prepared to take the helm.

—Hendrik Ibsen (1828-1906)

The world we live in has pretty much lost its moral high ground. There was a time when world leaders seemed to be guided by morality. Leaders like Susan B. Anthony, Abraham Lincoln, Mohandas Gandhi, Martin Luther King, and Nelson Mandela all seemed to do what was right at the time. In a real sense, greatness is not morality dependent. This is ably demonstrated in the likes of Al Capone and Hitler. People followed them even though their morality was suspect. More and more nations are cutting corners. Resultantly, their leaders lose integrity and subsequently corruption and fraudulent activities become the norm. History has taught us that dynasties, kingdoms, empires and civilizations decline from within and eventually disappear in the wake of moral decline.

Depending on one person to save the world is a hazardous practice. We need people from all walks of life, people with different experiences and perspectives, differing solution strategies and different realities. Tapping into the ideas of others increases the chances of finding solutions to our problems. We should at least tolerate and accept the idea that other people may harbor ideas that can complement one's incomplete picture of available solutions and possibilities. The diversity initiative hosts such possible solutions and makes it easier for people to work together. We will have more safeguards if we all commit to transparency, accountability, and a good conscience. Connectivity in today's corporate world is crucial. You need to connect with people across borders in spite of differences in order to energize the organizational mission. Whether you call it diversity, multiculturalism, or pluralism, the bottom line is that you have to work together as a group or remain duped by denial or the delusion of indulgence. You may think that you can survive on your own. However, diversity is a fact of our current business model. Diversity is thus better managed than mandated. You cannot force people to accept diversity; you can invite them though. The chances of finding solutions to our problems are increased exponentially if we at least tolerate and accept the idea that other people may harbor ideas that can complement one's incomplete picture of solutions and possibilities.

No one needs to feel uncomfortable in confronting diversity. Anyway, the world is in such a mess right now. You will know that many things are changing in society. People no longer talk about the sanctity of life but rather the quality of life. That moves the dialogue from a faith perspective to a scientific perspective. We have not fully realized what the fallout from this fundamental shift will be. We are however seeing more and more senseless crimes against people by people and by states violating the sovereignty of other states. The world has indeed become a fractured place that breeds estrangement between people in what was supposed to become a global village. Killing and violating people is meaningless to people who have not yet learned to respect the lives and property of others. In a quality of life world human flesh has becomes the cheapest commodity. Even our children no longer respect parents. Likewise people do not want to talk about diversity but rather inclusion and the engagement of all workers. That is okay as long as we do not ignore the real diversity issues. I see many organizations waking up to diversity initiatives because of the economy, violence in the workplace and risk management.

There is much role diffusion as well as role confusion in society. The gender specific role of mom and dad is blurring. Many dads have become housekeepers and care-givers while mom has become the breadwinner. Children have become confused by the changing parenting roles. This is true where one parent may have died or become absent because of divorce or separation. This is also true in second marriages. Mom and dad my try their best to focus on the children but the new marriage gets in the way. Mom may no longer be home on a fulltime basis because the economy forces her to work in order to augment the family income. These families may lack nothing but quality focused time. These young people will eventually enter the workplace with blank spaces in their developmental age and stage appropriate benchmarks. How does the workplace compensate for these missed opportunities early on, during childhood and adolescence? In the workplace it is not about therapy but training. Diversity training is one opportunity where the workplace can get in touch with human development by engineering an engaged workforce.

We hear and read about tragedy in everyday life almost everywhere we go. Just recently I was at the pharmacy and a woman was weeping because her girlfriend's sister had just committed suicide. Then there is the doctor who allegedly killed his nine year old son and three boys that set an 11 year old boy on fire because he failed to pay them for a video game. Teen on teen violence has become a category with alarming statistics. I have not even mentioned domestic violence and its impact on the workplace. These people are all connected to the workplace. Then there is the tragedy at Fort Hood, a military base steeped in patriotism. An army major who is also a psychiatrist killed 13 soldiers and one civilian. Is this tragedy at Fort Hood a product of "diversity ignorance" or disengagement in the workplace or of the emotional conflict of faith, patriotism and armed service or none of the above? How do we embrace people who come to work with long traditions and cultural constructs that are firmly etched in their mind-set? How do we transcend history? The world and our society are becoming more and more confused.

It reminds me of the boy who had the letters B. A. I. K. written on his tie. His teacher asked him what it meant and he replied that it meant "boy, am I confused". The teacher said that you do not spell confused with a "K". The boy replied, "Miss, you don't know how confused I am". In this confused and complex world we need to develop a diversity policy because a realistic diversity policy may prevent workplace disasters and promote authentic engagement. We have to rethink our diverse world that is being shaped by pain, trauma and greed.

Chilling economic crises, global warming crises, burgeoning human rights crises, and personal crises are spiraling out of control. It seems that these crises are growing in intensity, severity, and frequency. The world is experiencing the worst economic crisis since the Great Depression. Blaming or pointing fingers at one person or group does not undo the mess. No one person or group is going to put our precious world together again. We will have to learn to work together or we will certainly fall apart.

So many trivial things keep us from reaching out to each other in order to find solutions. What is it that prevents you from working with your fellow worker? Have you ever thought that that which you are finding deplorable in his or her life might simply be the reflection of what is deplorable in your own life? I suggest that you try to imagine the situation differently.

I define diversity as *the cooperative ofpeople who bring a variety of biological, spiritual and social backgrounds, styles, perspectives, values, and beliefs as assets to groups and organizations in which they work together to energize and enact the organizational mission.* The elementary act of recognizing diversity helps us to connect the great variety of gifts that people bring to the work and service of the organization. Diversity allows each of us to contribute in a special way to make our special gifts and talents a part of the collective effort.

Diversity efforts and programs in the workplace should be underpinned by the awareness that each one of us comes to this nexus of our personal lives and the lives of others in the workplace for different reasons and from different experiences. Like any aircraft that wants to land at a particular airport, the pilot has to communicate with the control tower. In typical language, the control tower will ask, the pilot what the attitude of the aircraft is to the runway. Based on this feedback, they jointly set a course of instruction and enactment to secure a safe landing, even under trying conditions. Likewise people come to this nexus and they try to make a smooth landing on these differing organizational runways. We may have been socialized, shocked, and shaped by a series of different events on the path of our lives. Like the pilot of an aircraft in final approach who has to take orders from the air traffic controller in the tower even if they do not like it, you have to submit to the directives of supervisors and managers in order to ensure a safe landing on the organizational runway. This is often a problem for us in the workplace. We do not want to take orders. When staff interacts with staff they advertise themselves and the past experiences of their lives.

Staff members have formal education and degrees. They have orientation training in the workplace. They get on-the-job in-service training. They are supervised, rewarded, and follow career paths and promotions. However, organizations are often not effective, efficient, and productive. Why? Because the greatest organizational asset, its human capital, is misunderstood and underutilized. We have to learn to understand our own behavior and relations in interactive-intensive organizations. We are okay while we are in bed asleep, but the minute we wake up and interact with others, we often go from peaceful existence to conflicted coexistence. Our abilities seem to be affected by interaction with others. The ability to make effective choices and live an authentic life depends to a great extent on our capability and capacity to be self-reflective. Self-reflection is the greatest asset that you have for living a fulfilling life that provides a sense of direction and influence over what happens to you. If you do not understand your own feelings, your own fears, your own values, your own intentions, and patterns of behavior, your life can be like a floater bobbing on the ocean and going nowhere. On a personal note, I had to be aware of the oppression that I was subjected to. I had to be aware that my physical movements were being dictated by a political regime that was bent on destroying any decency in the lives of people of color. I had to always be vigilant that the regime did not control my mind, my ideas and my freedom to think. They restricted my physical movements but they never succeeded in restricting my possibility thinking and solution strategies. People that have been incarcerated for a long time may be disconnected to the world that they are released in. So many things change while the incarcerated person is kept in the same space and time and a sort of mind freeze sets in. Many of them are so disconnected that soon after their release they may be back in prison. Likewise, people may try to join the diversity effort, may tolerate it for a while, get frustrated and eventually withdraw to their own comfort zone and circling the wagons, or laager mentality. Do not underestimate the power of mob mentality and people's need to follow whatever seems fashionable or hip. I am always fascinated by the swine mentality that often plays out in the workplace. Throw an ear of corn on the ground and if one pig runs to it, all the other pigs will follow. Now throw an ear of corn in another direction. The pigs will leave that ear of corn and run after what you have just thrown on the ground. It might not even be pig feed. Running after very new or different noise in the workplace underlines the fact that workers may not be effectively engaged.

Think about the gates that opened and the gates that closed on the journey of your life. You know how you felt at the time when you were either shut in or shut out. Have you thought of the possibility that for some unresolved reason you have remained at that gate spiritually while you are trying like hell to make it physically, mentally, and emotionally? Your energy is being sapped. Your body is here with me but your mind; well, in fact, you are where your mind is. Your attitude, your behavior reflects your thinking. What are you thinking? You come to work, you go home, you do your chores, you take care of your roles, tasks and responsibilities, but your life lacks passion. Why? It just does not make sense. It has no meaning, no purpose, and no spark. You are just not motivated anymore. Now you blame the manager. Blaming others robs you of energy; eventually you will be absent in your presence, fatigued by your own devices and constant defeats. So do not let your past and your professional arrogance dim the relevance of your humaneness.

Employees need to understand themselves better and relate to others more effectively. We all need to imagine our time at work as an adjustment of our lives in order to live our dreams. We do not have to agree with others in the workplace, but it helps.

The best way that leadership in business will understand the need for diversity is to help them see the connection between their products and services and the population groups they are targeting or are in need of their services. Organizations can actually effectively learn how to implement this. They will then be developing a relationship with their customers. Connectivity in today's corporate world is crucial. You need to connect with people across borders in spite of differences in order to energize the organizational mission. Whether you call it diversity, multiculturalism, or pluralism, the bottom line is that you have to work together as a group or team. Jonathan Smilansky, author of the report "The Systematic Management of Executive Talent," states that "business leaders and top executives normally recruit people who are like themselves. Leaders tend to hire and promote people who have similar career experiences and who have attended the same kind of universities and schools." This practice can be dangerous because it will be difficult to energize the organization and to reach the target market with a stale mind-set. This is particularly crucial to remember in an organization that is growing. In a typical organizational setting where the leadership employ people who think like they do, they often succeed in disengaging all the other employees who are not like them. This practice can have strengths and weaknesses. Managing diversity and managing the abilities of your talent pool are flip sides of the same coin or organizational initiative if you want your executive faces to mirror those of your trading spaces. Diversity plays a key role in strategic planning. Leonard Goodstein, Timothy Nolan, and J. William Pfeiffer (1992) remind us in *Understanding and Managing Diversity* that "strategic planning is the process by which the guiding members of an organization envision its future and develop the necessary procedures and operations to achieve that future." Fairness in an organizational setting is crucial. James Clawson (2006) states that "respect for a [manager] will lead that person to treat the employee with fairness and equality." Diversity entails creating a workplace worth working in for all, one that addresses power imbalances and in tandem with this seeks equal opportunities for all in the organization. Sketching, scenario building, and a general ability to envision and anticipate the future help the leader to inspire all followers to join the solutions quest. Diversity is thus better managed than mandated. Role playing can facilitate a comfort level where all can embrace diversity.

I just have to mention Nelson Mandela again in this context as we seek to embrace diversity:

> In its proper meaning equality before the law means the right to participate in the making of the laws by which one is governed, a constitution which guarantees democratic rights to all sections of the population, the right to approach the court for protection or relief in the case of the violation of rights guaranteed in the constitution, and the right to take part in the administration of justice as judges, magistrates, attorneys-general, law advisers and similar positions. In the absence of these safeguards the phrase "equality before the law," in so far as it is intended to apply to us, is meaningless and misleading. All the rights and privileges to which I have referred are monopolized by whites, and we enjoy none of them. The white man makes all the laws, he drags us before his courts and accuses us, and he sits in judgment over us. It is

> fit and proper to raise the question sharply, what is this rigid color-bar in the administration of justice? Why is it that in this courtroom I face a white magistrate, am confronted by a white prosecutor, and escorted into the dock by a white orderly? Can anyone honestly and seriously suggest that in this type of atmosphere the scales of justice are evenly balanced? Why is it that no African in the history of this country has ever had the honor of being tried by his own kith and kin, by his own flesh and blood? I will tell Your Worship why: the real purpose of this rigid color-bar is to ensure that the justice dispensed by the courts should conform to the policy of the country, however much that policy might be in conflict with the norms of justice accepted in judiciaries throughout the civilized world.

When you want to celebrate diversity, when you have a vision to make a difference and to bring about meaningful change, you will have to embrace a faith that can carry you through. Quitting the process is not an option. Just having opinions about life, family, and work is good. Opinions are the stuff that I hold but my convictions the stuff that holds me.

Chapter Ten

My Faith Looks Up

Unfortunately, many Americans live on the outskirts of hope—some because of their poverty, some because of their color, and all too many because of both. Our task is to help replace their despair with opportunity.

—President Lyndon B. Johnson's
inaugural address, January 8, 1964

In dealing with large-scale change, John and Doris Naisbitt talked about megatrends and Alvin and Heidi Toffler talked about waves where the first wave was the agricultural era, the second the industrial era, and the third the information age. Some of the things that I am witnessing in our world, at this time, are the collapse of economic giants like WorldCom, Enron, the mortgage and banking sectors, and the auto industry. I see infectious malignant greed at the core of this state of economic affairs. These collapsing economic giants have brought along some unintended consequences for equally greedy investors. People who were so sure of their future now need more than benign support and therapy. Why and how this was allowed to happen and why the regulators were asleep at the wheel will remain unanswered until we realize that we are all caught up in the economic tsunami of the fourth wave.

I see the world as post third wave. I see a fourth wave, the image or entertainment age. Currently, the entity or person that can entertain our needs best or more correctly who has the package that we perceive will suit our needs best, will get our resources. Buying the package seems so attractive and will seemingly save trouble and time while giving so much happiness. Once the real bill arrives or we are faced with the real cost, suicidal ideation seem to be an attractive antidote. Many people are caught up in this fantasy frenzy because the world has redeveloped an unquenchable thirst for the fantasy genre. I think that it is the fantasy element in the packaged deals that grips our imagination and pulls us into deals that we often cannot afford. The colorful advertising icons are attractive and informative and take a short cut to feeding our quest for information. We associate information with the color icons and logos. A big red circle means budget price, robust quality, and super value of Target Stores. A red ribbon signifies AIDS awareness. A black-and-white-checkered flag signifies winning in racing. Countries have a colorful flag that people salute and that energizes patriotism. All these changes and developments have indelibly etched a color code in the collective mind-set. The world we live in thrives on color coding, brand names and colors, icons and imagery. We the people seem to have a need to categorize, classify, color code, and order our world. In order to make sense of our world, we stipulate, we compartmentalize, we select and reject. Unfortunately we not just do this with things but with people too. We separate people by race, complexion, religion, and status.

America is the latest country to break the color-coded mold. Breaking this mold takes guts, conviction, faith, inspiration, motivation, empowerment, and commitment. The world has been building bridges across the racial divide. This is the era when we should be crossing the bridges in order to reconnect with others irrespective of their color, race, or religion. We should heal the world because color-coding people and harboring stereotypes have no place in this image or entertainment era. We should affirm all people irrespective of their color, race, or religion.

I am a survivor. I have only one life on this earth. My life is overflowing with positive energy. My life is tension-filled: a tension between my past experiences and my aspiration for the future. I have a brave hope that I will have enough time to get my message to young people. We should all be totally committed to preventative endeavors. Once a child has been abused, once a young person is suffering the consequences of their bad decision making, it increases the frequency and intensity of the need to help them to rework and to renegotiate their lives in order to stay on a positive development track. Child abuse and neglect are increasing and this is an indictment against a world that claims to be superior because of its great technological advances. Do you really know what it feels like to be abused as a child? Do you really know what it feels like to have no voice, no power and no safe place? Do you know what children are going though when the joy of their childhood is being disrupted? Do you know how overwhelming it is for a child to have no voice because the pain that the abused and/or neglected child is enduring is killing the child's ability to reach out for help? Do you know what it feels like to have no one claim you or take responsibility for you as a child? Do you know what it feels like to have nothing and to not even know that you can want something? Close your eyes, take a deep breath, hold your breath, and muse about these questions before you exhale. Do you know how many children still do not even have a name? The dismissive treatment of children and their issues is disgraceful in any language, culture, state, and country. As I rework the answers to the questions about my identity I am becoming excited about what my one life can contribute to society. More important however, is the question of what the meaning and purpose of my life is, and what people will remember me for. I believe that the colored people of South Africa went through a traumatic episode during the apartheid era. In South Africa and in America, I see so many people of color still being traumatized as a result of their living situation. Life for people of color can still be very hard simply because of their skin color. People still recoil on a color basis. Trauma, I have found in my work with abused young people, has the ability to derail, delay or develop capability and capacity. I have seen in their lives that if the trauma continues for a long period of time, it eventually frustrates and derails them. I have seen others who were traumatized and helped. However their vulnerability and exposure to risk had a significant impact on their ability to become functional again. Their developmental delays as they reworked and renegotiated their abilities were noticeable. The importance of a supportive, growth-producing relationship was vital in minimizing the delays caused by the trauma. Then there are those who, in spite of the trauma, were resilient and had other protective factors that mitigated the impact of the trauma to such an extent that they developed new capabilities and capacities. They overcame the trauma by becoming creative in how they negotiated life in the moment. When an individual is traumatized, help may be available in the form of peers, friends, relatives, and church groups. However, who will help if a society, group, or nation is traumatized? Who can help when even the institutions become tainted and contaminated as a result of the magnitude of the trauma?

Did my trauma make me doubt who I was? What made me doubt my roots, my rituals, my relationships, my reality, my religion? I have become who I am not because of apartheid but in spite of apartheid. My survival was possible because of my ability or resilience to overcome the odds coupled with key protective factors in my immediate environment. Resilience for me is the sum total of my positive innate ability in tandem with environmental protective factors that facilitated my overcoming of adversity. Emmy Werner and Ruth Smith (1992) talked about resilience as the potential to achieve positive life outcomes in spite of risk. Many people suffer as a result of the ideology, innuendo, and ill intent of others. The sad thing is that they, the perpetrators, the oppressors are often oblivious to the pain that their actions are causing others. I am using the term actions here because I like to think of behavior as an action or a series of actions. It is these actions or units of behavior that is my focus here. Sometimes we cannot fault others in their overall behavior but we can pinpoint suspect, overt or covert actions or even innuendo or other micro subtleties and inequalities.

We should move to create opportunities for people to see what they are doing to each other by their commission as well as omission. People are often not aware of the harm or pain they cause others. People who have been ill treated by others have gone on to save the life of their abusers. It does not happen often but it does. We constantly meet people. We do not always know who they are and what they may have endured. We distinguish between nice and nasty people. However, nice people can be nasty people depending on who they are, where they are and who their audience is. These demarcations are not all-exclusive or all-embracing. Many people are nicer to their animals and friends than to their own children, wives and family members. This is when I know the impact that the trauma may have had on their life. Trauma does leave a lasting impression on one's life. Trauma often defines who we are and is an ingredient that is mixed in with our identity. A white colleague of mine, a nice guy, whom I thought I was getting along with just fine in the workplace, surprised me one day. At work we would share breaks, hang out together and seeks each other's council. Well, one day my family and I went to the beach. One of my children pointed out that my colleague was down below on the beach. Excitedly, I started calling out to him but he just ignored my attention-seeking animations. He was with his real buddies, now. This kind of thing happens when people find more comfort within their own groups and betray relations that they may have with people in other dissimilar groups when they encounter them outside the usual context, such as the workplace. What do you do when people worship with you in the same church on Sunday and ignore you in the street on Monday? What do you do when people show their discomfort with being in your presence when their own buddies come along? There is really nothing you can do but just bite down hard and move along. In moments when people marginalized me and members of my group, we had to be sure of our identity and our right to exist. A world is emerging where we no longer have to question our existence; we need to affirm it all the time. I have to be sure of who I am. I have to be sure that identity is not just about my suffering and failure because identity includes achievements and aspirations. I have to be sure of my function and purpose in life. I have to be sure that my life has meaning in spite of those who claimed that my life was meaningless. I said earlier that my personal vision statement is *Deo Sevire Vera Libertas*, a Latin phrase that means I believe that I get my freedom from serving God. I do believe that there is a God. I do believe that He is real, that He is sovereign, and that He is in control. I believe that my life has meaning only in relation to God. I believe that He is a calm God, and the more I am aware of His presence, the less stressed and frantic I will be. In my saddest moments, in my worst, most painful experiences, I believed that God is the difference and that I am the difference and that together we can overcome. We are living in exciting times when more and more people are reexamining their mind-set, their prejudices, their stereotypes, even their own racism. I believe that we can only get to a nonracial society once there is no more overt and covert racism. This generation has to take racism by the horns and turn it around positively. It was important for me to have an *I-Thou* relationship because it ultimately gave meaning to my life. I have learned that I can stand on the promises of God. Even in those painful moments in my life when hope seemed impossible, when my reality was excruciatingly painful, I believed that God would reveal a way out to me. I did not know the details of His deliverance plans, I did not know the timing of His plans; but I did know that He would be true to His Word. How can I demonstrate the replacement of despair with opportunity?

- I will respect and affirm all people including those that are disrespectful, arrogant, indifferent, aloof, and antisocial in their manifest behavior. I will make every effort to encourage them and to help them learn to establish respectful, meaningful relationships with others.
- I will stop my wastefulness. I will make sure that I have a sufficient supply and reduce the waste of food, raw materials, stationery, and even clothing.
- I will take responsibility for the earth and its resources. I will participate in reclaiming lives and my environment.
- I will be the person that I want others to be. I will be the difference.

Ellen Key (1909) had visions of the twentieth century as the century of the child. Children are pretty much still part of the voiceless masses. "Children are our future," is only an aphorism unless we learn to treat children well. The children in the welfare system today will be in federal and state government by the time we go on pension, and they might just develop policies to punish us for not doing anything to help them heal their hurts and relationships in a humane manner and place. I see my function as that of the joker in a pack of cards. My function is determined by the need in a moment. The joker can be a replacement, a substitute, a second chance. I should be versatile, flexible, and consistent because sometimes people need me to be a medical doctor, nurse, teacher, friend, parent, sibling, and playmate. Sometimes I may even play the function of a punch bag or be the part of the puzzle that is missing. I have had to cook and counsel. I did this with love and joy, yet it was never about getting material rewards for these actions. It is accepted in today's business world that people are what set businesses apart from their competitors. Many studies provide proof that people factors are a major difference between high—and average-performing companies. Research shows that companies that enjoy the highest profitability in their industries are those that have invested in the development of the customer relationship management (CRM) of their workers.

What constitutes a customer? A customer has a

Connection with

Us in the organization. The customer wants a

Service or product within a specific

Time frame. This presents the

Opportunity for action. There needs to be a

Match between what the customer wants or needs and what we can provide. This whole process is

Evaluated by both parties who will determine whether to return for business. It is this

Return that defines one as a customer. Motivating and rewarding employees appropriately is thus of paramount importance if organizations want them to nurture and grow the customer base. Maslow's hierarchy of human needs deals with self-actualization. We know that we cannot self-actualize by playing a role. The notion for me is that the workplace is filled with people who are dissatisfied with themselves, and this leads to impoverished interpersonal relationships as well as intrapersonal relationships. The more people are satisfied, the more they ought to pursue satisfying others. This mind-set will serve diversity efforts very well. We are living in a multicultural world. We should be exposing all people to readings and discussion about concepts, frameworks and processes that may be useful in addressing human relations, diversity and multicultural issues facing educators and human services professionals. Topics, trends and themes to be covered should include: diversity training, racism, stereotyping, prejudice, "what's in it for me" (WIIFM), values, teamwork, learning styles theory, multiple intelligence theory, cultural bloopers, democracy, cultural self-analysis, cultural terminology and concepts, diversity implications, critical thinking skills cross-cultural communication, and the nexus of diversity, culture and the law. The objective would be to expose people to diversity and multicultural decision-making consciousness, dialogical competence and confidence, commitment to predetermined professional principles, and professional conduct in the workplace. A global blogging about race would indeed go a long way to facilitate an understanding of race and the feelings of people. We are survivors because the human spirit is tough and resilient and enormously adaptable under pressure. In spite of wars and conflicts, our chronicle remains replete with instances, large and small, of self-sacrifice and of dedication to others in the face of bleakness and terror. William James believed that "the community stagnates without the impulse of the individual. The impulse dies away without the sympathy of the community." Community is better "caught" than taught. We want to move from our professional comfort zones into the communal action zones. Community is not just a group of people located in the same neighborhood. Community implies sharing and involvement in communal values and cocreative activities as well as interaction in multiple contexts. Bad interpersonal relationships and a lack of communication skills often bedevil the striving for community. We lack quality in our communal interaction because we either do not engage authentically or we do not take ownership for our relationships. Remember that there is no joy without challenge. Friedrich Nietzsche was probably on target when he said that madness is rare in individuals—but in groups, parties, nations, and ages, it is the rule. We are witnessing ethnic violence and cleansing, fragmented communities, white-on-white and black-on-black violence. Why? It seems that nobody listened when Mahatma Gandhi said that no culture can live if it attempts to be exclusive. Perhaps English philosopher Thomas Hobbes (1588-1677) said it best when he said, "Men are continually in competition with one another for honor and dignity . . . Consequently there arises among men envy and hatred, and finally war." It is self-evident that people throughout the world cannot seem to get past their physical and uncontrollable differences to live together in a peaceful way. These problems of getting along not only affect the community in which they occur, but they also affect every other community. Globalization has made their problems our problems. Education is a pivotal component to economic prosperity because it also plays a crucial role in enabling people to improve the quality of their lives and contribute to a peaceful, productive and democratic nation. The health and development of children and adolescents is of vital importance. Yet young people face many health threats from diseases carried by food, water and soil, seasonal or permanent food shortages, and high risks of accidental injuries. AIDS has complicated this situation further by not only affecting thousands of children, but also causing thousands more to be orphaned at an early age. Did you know that 80 percent of all people who are HIV-positive are blacks and that 250,000 are dying of AIDS annually in South Africa? Preventable conditions such as malaria, diarrhea, acute respiratory diseases, and malnutrition are leading causes of morbidity in children under five years and they account for approximately 75 percent of the deaths in this age-group. Will you join with me in a quest to recall racism? Racism does not belong in our civilized world. It will take more than a strong resolve to tackle racism. Racism is caused by some and experienced by others. Racism in any shape or form is an unconscionable, inhumane and disgusting way of living your life, especially in the global village that is hurting so badly. This economic crisis has underlined the fact that we are all in this together. We are all hurting as a result of the greed of some. We all need to be engulfed by an epidemic of hope, support and camaraderie. In any nation where racism is thriving, we are all losers, whether we are the exploiter-losers or the exploited-losers. In the short term, racism may look like a good thing, but in the long run, we lose. You cannot reach the goal of a nonracial society if you leave racism unchecked. You cannot be a coward if you want to tackle racism head-on. Racism has to be confronted personally. Racism has to be recalled by you! Even the de facto majority of your group is not a license to be racist.

Racism refers to certain "superior" attitudes and actions of some people that in some way disadvantage other people on the basis of their deemed-to-be "inferior" race. This negative value judgment is both morally wrong and indefensible because of its intentions and its consequences. You may have grown up with racism. Racism may have been entrenched by the attitude of your parents, your synagogue, your church, your mosque or your school, your college, or your primary system. So much so that racism "happens" subconsciously. However, whatever your background, only you are ultimately responsible for your racism. We need to revisit the way individuals interact with others. Just take a look at the courtesies we bestow upon one other. We need to just observe how downright rude we can be to one another especially in public spaces. I have often come away from these observations with the conviction that I could see nothing else at play but racism. When someone literally pushes you out of line at a ticket booth or at the grocery store it is appalling, and even more so if that person is from another race. I have had many encounters with racists. One that stands out is what happened on a flight from Charlotte to Phoenix. The gentleman (of another race) took the magazine and placed it between my shoulder and his shoulder and he actually requested that I should not touch him. Wow! Racial categories appear biological but have an impact on social interactions and sanctions. Racial categories in the United States often appear mutually exclusive but may in fact be overlapping. Right now you can be African-American, Native American, and Caribbean-American. Some countries, such as the United States, have elected a first African-American president while the undertones and overtones of race still play out in others like South Africa where race remains an obstacle given the election results of the 2009 election. Yet racism persists in America too. We need to look at racism in the institutions of our society. The quality of the interactions between people is a good barometer of the racism inherent in society. If you have an organization whose management consists of only one race and the workers are comprised of all the other races, then something is amiss. Why are minorities not allowed in the power sharing and management of the institution and/or organization? We need to look at promotions and career ladders because often racism is the glass ceiling that prevents people from upward mobility. We need to look at the social and institutional structures that disadvantage groups by denying them access because of their race. We need to look at institutionalized racism or racism that is so entrenched in the way society operates that it becomes normative. Racism has a long history and as such has seemingly benefited some while definitely denying opportunities to others. No legislation or act of congress can undo what has been done and approved by governments and institutions under the banner of racism. No-one can erase the pain suffered as a result of racism. And, we need to do something more than agree that racism is wrong. We need to engage in exploratory dialogues about race. Definitely, a national truth and reconciliation exercise can lead the nation to understanding and forgiveness en route to reconciliation and national rebuilding efforts. We need to resolve to not allow people to make racist jokes or remarks in our presence. If there is not an ear to listen, there will not be a tongue to whisper. We need to be aware of our own racism, prejudice and stereotyping. We need to unlearn old habitual ways of interacting with other races, and if need be, seek counseling to learn new ways of interaction. Do something about the recall of racism, now. After all is said and done, more is said than done. God forbid. I call on you to join a collective effort to make a difference to the "flatline" neighborhoods nearest to you—or it may even be the one that you are living in. A flatline neighborhood occurs when the risk elements in a neighborhood annihilate the protective, positive elements. Crime, abuse, domestic violence, drug abuse, alcohol abuse, unemployment and inadequate infrastructure and resources will exacerbate the impact of the risk factors and eventually result in a flatline neighborhood. Campus and workplace violence and threats of violence are all symptomatic of the fragmentation of the sense of community and the emergence of the flatline culture. Killings on university and college campuses seem to be the new wave of intellectual and smart terrorism. You know what issues and actions will further traumatize children and youth. Get a group of volunteers that are passionate about children and youth to develop ideas that can bring back the pulse, energy or heartbeat to these neighborhoods. Get the youth to do community service projects. I had an at-risk youth group run a soup kitchen for homeless people. On another occasion I had a diverse group of young people participate in the *bone strategy*. This is a strategy that helps a group to define a single value as a binding force for the group. You ask a group of twenty or more young people to commit to a three-hour interactive-intensive workshop. Each one has to bring something that they value as special, to the session. One after the other, they will hold up this symbol, explain why they value it and why it should be respected by others. After this initial round someone else in the group can take that symbol and "floor" it. When a symbol is floored, it cannot be restored by the owner. It has to be redeemed by someone else. Symbols can be floored and restored multiple times. Eventually only one symbol will be most valuable to the group. Emotions will flare and frustration will become evident. The past pain and rejection suffered by the participants will initially drive the process. However, with great facilitation the group will learn the value of respect for others. The more the group communicates with each other the more objective they will become. The more they learn about each other, the more they will trust each other. Do not be afraid to take risks and to step out of your comfort zone because we need an army of people who are passionate about changing the world. Why are you and I still here? We have survived to be the living difference. The next book that I will be reading is the narrative of your life, your efforts and your loyalty to leaving a lasting legacy. Will you be the change you want to create?

I am detecting an awkward restlessness in the world. It is as if oppressed peoples in many countries are poised for an uprising. People seem to be fed up with the status quo and it's seemingly never ending struggles and hardships. Many young people are tired of seeing their parents struggle to make ends meet. Many parents are tired of not having enough to share with their children. People want change. People want release from the yoke of oppression. People want to revolutionize the biased social order. People want to live. People can only live if their brave hope can materialize in a better day for all people.

This is the time for change and the time is now when everybody is waiting with bated breath for the birth of the new order. People are growing impatient with leaders who promise change but cannot deliver. Maybe, just maybe a major shake-up in the world can begin with you and I treating our neighbors with respect and making this world a better place. Are you willing to share what you have in order to lift the load that is currently overwhelming your neighbor? You can be a world changer. You can be the provider of the different day that abused children are dreaming about. You can make the difference in the lives of parents and young people who have no access to opportunities. You can bring healing, wholeness and hope to many people who are not well.

Will you be an energizer? Will you be an encourager? Will you engage others to be the difference? Will you commit to flatline change?

The Grateful Life is Preserved

God is so good to me all the time
Why I am so special has neither reason nor rhyme
My love is more concrete than faith and hope
I engage all with kindness even at the end of their rope
If we can keep our dreams alive
Obstacles will fade and inspire stewardship's will to survive

If I have strength I owe the service of the strong
If melody I have I owe the world a song
If I can keep my head when all around my space are falling
If I can run with speed when needy hearts are calling
If my torch can light the dark of any night
Then I must pay the debt I owe with living light

If heavens grace has endowed me with some rare gift
If I can lift some load no other's strength can lift
If I can heal some wound no other's hand can heal
If some great truth the logos to me reveal
Then I must go a broken a wounded thing
If to a wounded world my gifts no healing bring

For any gift God gives to me I cannot pay
Gifts are really mine when I give them all away
God's gifts are like His flowers that show their right to stay
By giving all their bloom and fragrance away
Riches are not in gold, land, estate or mart
The only wealth worth having is in the human heart

Recommended Reading

Ashkanasy, N. M., Hartel, C. E., and C. S. Daus. 2002. Diversity and emotion: The new frontier in organizational behavior research. *Journal of Management* 28 (3): 307-338.

Badgett, W. O. 2007. Criteria for ethics assessments. *Internal Auditor* 64 (1): 65-69.

Belasco, W. 1990. Appetite for change: How the counterculture took on the food industry and what happened when it did. New York: Knopf Publishing Company.

Bennis, W. 1994. On becoming a leader. Reading, MA: Addison Wesley.

Bennis, W., and J. Goldsmith. 1997. Learning to lead: A workbook on becoming a leader. Reading, MA: Perseus Books.

Bolman, L.G. and Deal, T.E. 2008. Reframing organizations. 4th edition. San Francisco, CA: Jossey Bass.

Brady, T. 1996. The downside of diversity. *HR Focus* 73 (8), 22-2.

Brannon, P. M. 2004. Diversity. *Human Ecology* 32 (1): 1.

Chowdhury, S. 2000. Management 21C. New York: Prentice Hall.

Clawson, J. G. 2006. Level three leadership: Getting below the surface. 3rd edition. Upper Saddle River, New Jersey: Prentice Hall, 72-73.

Dreachslin, J. L. and F. Hobby. 2008. Racial and ethnic disparities: Why diversity leadership maters. *Journal of*

Healthcare Management 53 (1), 8-13. Retrieved August 7, 2008, from ABI/INFORM Global Database. (Document ID: 1422398451).

Farrell W. 2001. The myth of male power. New York, NY. Berkley Publishing Group.

Frankl, V. 1988. Man's search for meaning: An introduction to logotherapy. New York: Pocket Books.

Goodstein, L. D., Nolan, T. M., and J. W. Pfeiffer. 1992. Applied strategic planning: A comprehensive guide. San Diego, CA: Pfeiffer & Co.

Gravett, Linda. 2001. Why diversity training fails. *e-hresources.* Retrieved August 7, 2008, from *www.eihresources.com/Articles/Aug2001.htm.*

Harvey, C. P., and M. J. Allard. 2009. Understanding and Managing Diversity. 4th ed. Upper Saddle River, NJ. Pearson Prentice Hall.

Heifetz, R. 2003. Leadership without easy answers. Cambridge, MA: Harvard University Press.

Kouzes, J. M., and B. Z. Posner. 2002. The leadership challenge. New York: Jossey-Bass.

Kuczmarski, S., and T. Kuczmarski. 2002. Values-based leadership: Rebuilding employee commitment, performance, and productivity. Collingdale, PA: Diane Publishing Company.

Mandela N. R. 1964. "I am prepared to die." Statement from the dock at the opening of the defense case in the Rivonia trial Pretoria Supreme Court, April 20, 1964. Retrieved May 16, 2004, from http://www.anc.org.za/ancdocs/history/rivonia.html.

McCauley, C. D., and E. Van Velsor. 2004. Handbook of leadership development. 2nd ed. San Francisco: Jossey Bass, 45, 119, 161, 449-450.

McDonough, M. 2005. Demanding diversity. *ABA Journal* 91 (March): 52-57.

Medina, H. 2008. The current state of diversity in the workplace. *Hispanic Business* 30 (62): 62-64.

Meyer, C. F., and E. K. Rhoades. 2006. Multiculturalism: Beyond food, festival, folklore, and fashion. Kappa Delta Pi Record 42 (2): 82-87. Retrieved August 7, 2008 from WilsonWeb database.

Mitchell, L. 2005. Impacting teacher candidates' knowledge, skills, and dispositions regarding diversity: Faculty triggers. *Journal of Thought* 40 (3): 91-106. Retrieved August 7, 2008, from ProQuest Social Science Journals database. (Document ID: 909637601).

Nancheria, A. 2008. Why diversity training doesn't work . . . Right now. *Journal of Training and Development* 62 (11): 52-59.

Point, S., and V. Singh. 2003. Defining and dimensionalising diversity: Evidence from corporate websites across Europe. *European Management Journal* 21 (6): 750-761.

Rubenstein, D. 2008. Guidelines to achieving diversity. *Modern Healthcare* 38 (10): 48.

Senge, P. 1990. The fifth discipline: Mastering the five practices of the learning organization. New York: Doubleday.

Sergiovanni, T. J. 1999. Rethinking leadership: A collection of articles. Arlington Heights, Illinois: Skylight Professional Development.

Triandis, H. 1993. Culture and social behavior. London: McGraw-Hill Series in Social Psychology.

Yukl, G. 2002. Leadership in organizations. 5th ed. New Jersey: Prentice Hall.

Index

C

L

M

N

O

P

R

S

T

About the author

Dr. Michael W. G. Gaffley, CYC-P, is proficient in the art and science of paradigm shifts, relational education, and lifestyle negotiations in diverse contexts. He is a certified child and youth care practitioner and is a board member of the Association for Child and Youth Care Practice Inc. and a member of the Child and Youth Care Certification Board. He worked with sexually, physically, and emotionally abused children and youth and with socially excluded families in high-risk environments. He is a former executive director of state and NGO agencies in South Africa where, for more than twenty years, he was a driving force in many collaborative community-based partnerships. He worked with the Mandela government to implement social, political, and economic change. During this transformation process, from apartheid to democracy, he developed Organizabonding, a leadership and organizational capability and capacity building, education, training, and technical assistance model facilitating the comprehensive management of the human capital investment in human services organizations. Repositioning, reframing, and relating with people to celebrate diversity in organizations is his forte. He has keynoted, presented, and inspired at various national and international child-and-youth-focused conferences around the world. He is the recipient of numerous meritorious and academic awards for his accomplishments in difficult times, among others, Outstanding Student Achievement Award from NSU, Mayoral and Chairman's commendations, and the WC Provincial Government's commendation for leadership during the transformation process. Michael brings the quintessential pinnacle perspective; he educates, informs, and agitates.

Get Published, Inc!
Thorofare, NJ 08086
04 February, 2010
BA2010035